Equal Opportunity and Equal Pay

a review of objectives, problems and progress

G J Mepham

Institute of Personnel Management
5 Winsley Street, Oxford Circus, London W1N 7AQ

First published 1974

© Institute of Personnel Management
No part of this publication may be reproduced in any form
without written permission

ISBN 085292 096 2

Set in 10pt Times

The passages from *Family Policy* by Margaret Wynn,
Penguin 1972, are reproduced by permission.

The material reproduced in the appendices from the
Government publications cited is Crown copyright and is
reproduced by permission of the Controller of Her
Majesty's Stationery Office.

Printed in Great Britain
by Seel House Press

Acknowledgements

The views expressed in this book, apart from the two statements from the Institute, are my own. I am indebted, however, to those many friends and colleagues who have helped me to formulate these views over the years.

G J Mepham

February, 1974

The author is Remuneration Manager in a group of companies in the light electrical and electronics industry.

Contents

1 Introduction and IPM Statements

In the course of preparing this book, I have repeatedly been aware of how closely inter-related are the social, economic and cultural problems raised by changes in the United Kingdom's employment structure that have occurred since the 1940s. Measures to alleviate one problem will probably add to difficulties of another kind, but often a move towards a solution on one problem will reduce the significance of another. Every move should therefore be seen and planned as part of a broadly-based strategy.

My conclusion from writing and thinking about the demand for equal opportunity and equal pay is that we need, as part of such a broadly-based strategy, to end the division of the labour market as quickly as we can. Change of the order we are concerned with is never easily achieved, but hesitation and uncertainty are of little gain when it is evident, as here, that change is long overdue. The need for legislation on both equal pay and equal opportunity is now generally accepted but legislation alone cannot satisfy the demands for change. Attitudes and assumptions must change and determined efforts be made to find realistic and acceptable solutions to the problems of implementing change.

My purpose in writing this book has been to make a small contribution to this process of education and persuasion. Readers will quickly discover that chapters 3, 4 and 5 are largely devoted to a statistical analysis of the situation in education, training and employment. The following chapters examine the changes needed to facilitate the employment of women and to enlarge their opportunities, in particular on their return to work after bringing up a family. The final short chapter lists urgent points of action required to remedy the situation. These chapters are preceded by two IPM policy statements, *Women and Employment* and *Equal Opportunities for Men and Women*. The first is the IPM's policy statement and the second is the Institute's considered comment on the Government's consultative document setting out proposals on equal opportunities for men and women (see p 89).

In several chapters, a number of reports have been quoted. In the text these have been referred to by abbreviated titles as follows:

The Select Committee

House of Lords, Select Committee on the Anti-Discrimination Bill

The House of Commons Sub-Committee

House of Commons, Sub-Committee (on the Employment of Women) at the Expenditure Committee

The House of Commons Expenditure Committee

House of Commons. Expenditure Committee which reported on the Sub-Committee's findings

The Departmental Committee

Committee set up to report on The Employment of Women in the Non-Industrial Civil Service

(Other abbreviations in the text are listed in Appendix 33)

For the purposes of this book, I have accepted the definition of discrimination adopted by the Select Committee:

"Treatment of an individual, on grounds of sex, less favourably than other individuals".

Women and employment

Policy statement by the Institute of Personnel Management

1 General background

1.1 Equality for women may be said to be one of the most important social issues of the day. The movement which seeks to change fundamentally the social role of women may at present be in the hands of a vocal minority group of educated women but it is gradually gaining ground.

As with any major change, deep rooted traditions and attitudes are not easily or quickly overcome but there are signs that mounting pressure from the movement will be a feature of the 70s. Nor will it abate until the problems of sex discrimination have been finally resolved.

1.2 This situation is reflected in the growing pressure for legislation. A private member's bill on sex discrimination has repeatedly been brought before the house since Mrs Joyce Butler's original bill in 1968. These efforts culminated in 1972 with the bill presented by William Hamilton, MP for West Fife, which sought to make unlawful discrimination in employment and education on grounds of sex. Although talked out of the House of Commons on its second reading, it had in the meantime been taken up in the House of Lords, and in June 1972, the Institute presented written and oral evidence to the special House of Lords Select Committee which had been set up on the Anti-Discrimination (No 2) Bill. In its evidence the Institute declared its belief in the need for such legislation although it had reservations about the Bill as it stood and would like to have seen broader legislation introduced to ensure equal treatment for men and women, in particular changes in the existing Factories Act and Social Security laws.

1.3 Since then the House of Lords has sifted a considerable amount of evidence and has produced its own version of the Anti-Discrimination Bill, renamed the Sex Discrimination Bill. The Government in turn has declared its intention to produce legislation of its own. This, combined with increasing public interest and signs of growing militancy at least among certain groups of women, makes it probable that some form of sex discrimination legislation will appear on the Statute Book within the next two years.

1.4 In the meantime much could be achieved by forward looking employers and personnel directors to eliminate discrimination on the ground of sex in their own organizations and to make the best use of their womanpower. In so doing, they would also be making the maximum use of human resources – a matter of primary concern to personnel managers. At present this country is wasting much of these resources at a time when it can ill afford to do so.

1.5 It is not only uneconomic to permit the continued waste or misuse of womanpower, it is also clearly unjust. In the past the majority of companies have perhaps not been over concerned with matters of social justice but now that companies are coming under increasing pressure to consider their social responsibilities it may be wise for boards of directors to submit their employment policies and practices to closer scrutiny. If they find themselves suddenly exposed to the glare of publicity on such issues as their treatment of women it will not be enough to plead ignorance.

2 Affirmative action

2.1 Even if legislation is passed, a policy of non-discrimination will not be sufficient in itself to improve the position of women. Declarations of non-discrimination are easily made and as easily forgotten. The Institute urges companies to adopt affirmative action programmes for equality at work between the sexes and suggests the following steps which can be taken to implement such a programme.

Top management commitment

2.2 Obtain the commitment of top management. This is the essential first step in any affirmative action programme.

2.3 In setting out to obtain top level commitment, prepare an estimate of the costs involved since no board will wish to decide on such a policy without knowing what it will cost. Ensure that figures are based on known facts and not on common assumptions about women at work which may well be false.

2.4 Issue a policy statement – top management commitment must be demonstrated by a written statement of policy signed by the chairman or managing director and distributed to all levels throughout the organization. At the same time a member of senior management, probably the personnel director, should be given responsibility for planning the programme and monitoring its implementation. Remember that a policy statement alone is not worth the paper it is written on without appropriate follow-up action.

Communcating the policy

2.5 After circulating the policy statement, organize group discussion meetings of managers and supervisors to explain the policy and outline the affirmative action programme. This will enable problems to be brought into the open and may help to break down resistant attitudes.

2.6 Similarly, if your company is unionized, engage the support of all unions concerned by consulting with branch officials and shop stewards at the earliest possible stage. This is vital as no change programme will get off the ground without union involvement. Other means of communication can include notice boards, a feature in the house journal and special brochures.

Recruitment

2.7 Carry out an investigation of all jobs in the organization to ascertain which could genuinely not be undertaken by a woman and which could not be undertaken by a man. The reasons must genuinely be based upon sex differences and not upon preconceived assumptions about women (or men) at work. Jobs of this kind would fall into a special category for which sex is defined as a genuine occupational requirement.*

* In the United States such jobs are known as BFOQ (ie jobs for which sex is a Bona Fide Occupational Qualification) and are very narrowly defined. Thus sex has been accepted as a BFOQ for modelling clothes, for lavatory attendants and for underwear sales assistants. Furthermore, the burden of proof rests with the employers or unions to justify their action in excluding one sex or the other.

2.8 Avoid the use of discriminatory wording in job advertisements.

2.9 Advertise all vacancies internally as this will give existing female employees the opportunity to apply.

2.10 Design careers literature to show equal opportunities for young men and women. Do *not*, for example, illustrate management trainee brochures with pictures of bright young men dictating to their clearly subordinate female secretaries.

2.11 Work with all educational institutions from whom you draw applicants to encourage women to obtain qualifications and to apply for jobs with your company.

2.12 Inform employment agencies that *all* qualified applicants (men or women) should be put forward for the relevant jobs. Similarly inform selection consultants that your organization wishes to select the best candidate whether male or female.

2.13 Check that all those concerned with recruitment (men and women) are fully aware of the affirmative action programme.

2.14 Check that women are being recruited for jobs at all levels including managerial levels. Where you find, for example, that few, if any, are being recruited to the higher job categories, a more detailed investigation is clearly called for.

Training
2.15 Review training schemes at all levels in the company to ensure that they are open to men and women alike. Particular attention should be paid to craft apprenticeships and day release facilities for young women. Training is the key to equal opportunity. Many jobs are barred to women because they lack the necessary training but frequently this is due, in turn, to the fact that they have been barred from training schemes. Too often it has been

thought uneconomic to train women because of their alleged high labour turnover and absenteeism. All evidence suggests that turnover and absenteeism is highest among women in what Herzberg would describe as Mickey Mouse jobs, which are predominantly occupied by women; qualifications, skill and responsibility encourage women to remain for longer periods in their jobs. Similarly, research has shown that labour turnover is not as high among older women returning to work.

2.16 Check that women are being trained and developed both by participating in appropriate training courses either internal or external and by other development activities such as job rotation, planned experience and coaching.

2.17 Be prepared to take late entrants (ie older men and women) into your training schemes. There are common assumptions about age limits for training which operate against men and women but particularly against women because of their interrupted career patterns.

2.18 Allow for the possible need to make special training arrangements for women returning to employment after breaks in their careers. They may be nervous about re-entering industry and could be helped by
   (1) Appropriate induction procedures
   (2) Re-training to meet the needs of industry which may have changed during their absence
   (3) Participating in TOPS (the Government Training Opportunity Scheme) or other external training, preferably with the employer's guarantee of engagement on successful completion of the training. It is essential, however, that women do not limit themselves and are not limited by such schemes to be trained for sex stereotyped jobs.

Job enrichment
2.19 Consider the introduction of job enrichment/work

structuring programmes where applicable. These would apply to both men and women but since it is often the women who are in the least satisfying jobs they might be expected to benefit more.

Promotion

2.20 Analyse the career patterns over a period of men and women recruited at the same time and with similar qualifications. Compare the relative positions of the men and women, taking into account performance appraisal reports for all concerned.

2.21 Review your present system for appraising performance and identifying potential to ensure that it has no sex bias.

Review of total programme

2.22 Monitor the progress of your affirmative action programme through reports on all aspects, eg female recruitment, promotion of women and numbers of women participating in training and development programmes.

2.23 Report on results for the year to top management; review results and consider future action with them. Do not be surprised or disheartened if progress is slow, particularly in promotion. The fact that the chairman has seen the light of equal opportunity will not produce a crop of budding female executives overnight. Constant neglect in the past will not have produced fertile ground and the short term results may well be disappointing. It is the long term effects of affirmative action that are really important.

3 Conditions of employment and social security

3.1 In the United States affirmative action programmes similar to that outlined have been introduced in companies against the background of equal opportunity legislation. While we have seen that much can be done by employers without the backing of legislation there are certain important issues affecting women at work in this country which require action by Government.

3.2 The Equal Pay Act which comes into force in 1975 seeks to eliminate discrimination between men and women in pay and other terms and conditions of employment. This it does by establishing the right of women to equal treatment when they are employed on work of the same or broadly similar nature as men, or when they are employed on work which has been given equal value under a job evaluation scheme. However, and this is important, statutory control of women's hours or work, retirement age and pensions do *not* fall within the scope of the Act.

Hours of work

3.3 The Institute urges that if the Government is to introduce sex discrimination legislation it must at the same time repeal those sections of the Factories Acts which class adult women with young persons as needing special protection.

3.4 Legal restrictions on hours of work for women were introduced in 1844 when they were no doubt highly necessary. Today these restrictions apply only to women manual workers in premises covered by the Factories Acts and include a limit of 48 hours per week which must not start before 7 am or end after 8 pm. Employers can apply for exemptions from these rules if they have the agreement of the workers' organization concerned. Domestic circumstances will of course influence a woman's decision whether or not to work night shifts or overtime but the Institute sees no reason why women should not be allowed to decide for themselves what is good for them and have the same freedom as men to determine by agreement with their employers what their hours of work should be.*

---

*In the past TUC representatives have argued in favour of keeping restrictions because a large proportion of working women are married and therefore it is said that they are subject to pressures which are likely to cause them to overwork against their better judgement. Thus the TUC has argued that the State must intervene to protect women against the combined effect of social and economic pressures. This argument is put forward particularly strongly with respect to night work. However, the views of trade unionists on night work for women are divided and opinions vary from one industry and from one part of the country to another. The general TUC attitude may well change once equal pay is fully implemented.

3.5 The Institute, however, upholds the view expressed by the United Nations "that measures taken to protect women in certain types of work, for reasons inherent in their physical nature, should not be regarded as discriminatory".*

Flexible working hours
3.6 Some of the problems which women encounter in running a home and a job may be eased by the introduction of flexible working hours which give employees an element of choice in their starting and finishing times. According to an IPM survey of the subject the system is particularly favoured by married women.†

Social security

3.7 The Institute regrets that the Government has failed to adopt a more modern view of the social role of women. The 1973 Social Security Act continues the concept of sexual inequality and the assumption that women will be supported by men.

3.8 In particular the Institute urges the Government to equalize statutory conditions relating to national insurance for men and women in similar circumstances and to study the implications of introducing continuous insurance cover for women bringing up families at home.

Retirement age

3.9 A most important factor which militates against women at present, both in state and occupational pensions, is the differential in retirement age for men and women. The retirement age for women should be the same as that for men whether it be at 60, 63 or 65. The present retirement age for a woman at 60 means that her pension may be further reduced since she is denied the extra five years' accrual granted to men. This is particularly important in

*Article 10 of the *Declaration on the Elimination of Discrimination Against Women*, United Nations
† *Flexible Working Hours*, Information Report 12. J M Hill, IPM 1972

occupational schemes based on final salary, especially in a period of heavy inflation.

Pensions

3.10 The proposed new State Reserve Scheme and indeed most current occupational pension schemes assume that, since women live longer on the average than men and therefore draw pensions for longer, they should receive lower pensions. This in fact means that, since women are at present forced to retire earlier, they must endure their old age for longer and on less money than men. The Institute urges the Government to reconsider these principles and stop treating men and women as separate species for retirement and pension purposes.

3.11 Equal pension rights should be available to women. At present, considerable disparities between the treatment of men and women are to be found in many occupational pension schemes. These include minimum age of joining and qualifying period of service. Such discrimination should be abolished.

3.12 Even where schemes offer virtually the same terms for men and women, one major problem in existing schemes lies in failure over the provision for dependents. For example, while many schemes provide for a widow's pension, few if any have a widower's pension. The Institute recommends that dependents' allowances should be equally available to men and to women depending on their contributions and not on their sex.

Maternity leave

3.13 The present practice in private industry is to make no special provision for maternity leave for employees. Indeed both employer and employee have tended to assume that the woman will resign. The public sector however provides examples of various schemes, further details of which are included in Appendix 1 together with the TUC recommendations on the subject and a brief review of European practice. Changes in the pattern of employment and social security such as are recommended in this paper may affect both individual decisions about return to work after the birth of a child and company views on reinstatement. At this stage, the Institute is aware of strong views against the introduction either of guaranteed re-employment (without paid leave) or any form of company payment. However, there is scope for careful re-examination of the assumptions on which existing policies have been based, bearing in mind the need to move towards harmonization with EEC practices.

Day nurseries

3.14 The provision of day nursery facilities is essential for mothers who are obliged to carry on full time work and an incentive for those who wish to do so. The Institute recommends that local authorities be given financial encouragement to extend nursery services. It does not consider that the provision of such facilities falls within the responsibility of employers although, clearly, certain companies may find it necessary to provide their own day nurseries, particularly if they wish to attract women in areas of difficult recruitment.

4 Women in personnel management

4.1 In its evidence to the House of Lords Select Committee the Institute reported that it had found widespread discrimination in its own profession. Reports from colleges preparing students for IPM examinations often suggest that women do better than men on courses and frequently gain distinctions in examinations results. At this stage of their careers therefore it may be said that women do as well as men, if not better. Thereafter, however, women are overtaken by men and in fact very few women are to be found in senior appointments in personnel management.

4.2 Too many employers tend to see women in recruitment

(particularly clerical recruitment), training or industrial welfare jobs but not in industrial relations, manpower planning or the higher ranks of salary administration. Far too few young women in personnel departments are receiving the practical training and development that is required for these jobs. Yet it is only by having the right mix of skills and experience that women can break through into the higher levels of personnel management. It is a sad indictment of personnel managers that they who preach management development to line managers appear to have such a poor record of developing their own female subordinates.

4.3 The position of women in personnel management simply reflects the position of women in management generally. However, Institute members have a special responsibility here. Encouragement should be given to women to obtain practical experience in such areas as industrial relations and manpower planning.* Much more attention should be paid to *planned* career development for young women in personnel work and to the special development needs of older women returning to the field after a break in their career. For their part, women should stop accepting the role of clerical recruiters and start pressing for better opportunities.

4.4 The Institute itself through its Appointments Service and Membership and Student Services Departments is already doing what it can to promote equal opportunity for women. The Appointments Service, for example, already tries to persuade all advertisers to drop discriminatory wording on grounds of sex in advertisements published in *Personnel Management* and the *IPM Digest*. However, there is a limit to what it can do particularly at the moment without the backing of legislation. It is for this reason that the Institute urges action from members

* For example, what is to prevent women being trained as negotiators? ASTMS have done this with considerable success.

14

in individual companies. It is only by action and commitment from members that the Institute can achieve any concrete results on this important issue.

5 Conclusion

5.1 The Institute appreciates that, even if all the proposals it has made were implemented tomorrow, it is unlikely that any marked increase in the numbers of women in responsible positions would be achieved in this generation, or possibly in the next. Research has shown that sex role stereotyping begins when a child is given its first doll or toy soldier and is continued throughout the all important formative years. We have a long way to go towards educating men *and* women that, given equal opportunity, women can be as efficient as men in jobs of authority. Nevertheless, this should not deter us from action now. The position of women in the future will depend to a considerable extent on the *present* commitment of Government, managements, trade unions and social institutions alike to the principles of equality and to active policies aimed at the elimination of all forms of discrimination on the ground of sex.

Appendix 1

Maternity leave

There are two schools of thought on the provision of maternity leave among advocates of equal opportunity. On the one hand there are those who believe companies should establish a generous system of maternity leave and benefits to encourage women to return to work after child bearing. On the other hand there are those who would argue that maternity leave could reduce job opportunity for women, since employers might be reluctant about placing a woman in a skilled job if they knew they had to keep it open for her for three months or more while she was away having a baby.

Some would also argue that it is socially undesirable to encourage mothers to take full-time employment while leaving their babies with relatives or au pairs.

TUC recommendations

There is mounting pressure from trade unions for employers to grant maternity leave. Late in 1971 the TUC general council drew the attention of affiliated organizations with women members to examples of "best practice in the public sector maternity leave arrangements". In order to match up on all counts the TUC suggested that any new agreements concluded should:

(a) cover all women workers with more than 12 months service whether married or not;
(b) grant 18 weeks leave; 11 weeks before confinement and seven weeks after;
(c) give full pay for four weeks and half pay for 14 weeks;
(d) exclude maternity leave from calculations about future sick pay entitlement;
(e) Include restrictions designed to ensure that the woman resumes work after maternity leave; but with the right of appeal to a joint union management body.
(f) Contain restrictions to protect the new mother's health when she returns to work plus an allowance for paid leave so expectant mothers can go to ante-natal clinics without loss of pay.

Public sector

In the public sector maternity leave arrangements are fairly common. For example, in the Civil Service an established woman civil servant is allowed three months leave on full pay for a confinement which is reckoned against her normal sick pay entitlement. The first two months are paid when they fall due but the third month is not paid until the woman has completed three months service after her return to work. She may have further sick leave within her normal entitlement for as long as may be necessary provided a medical certificate is produced. In future under a new agreement concluded with the staff side unestablished staff will receive the same entitlement as established staff subject to a qualifying period of one year's service.

In local authority services women officers are granted maternity leave on the basis of four weeks full pay less national insurance benefits and 14 weeks on half pay without deductions but such leave is not counted against sick leave entitlement. The electricity, gas and water supply industries have somewhat similar arrangements, and staff employed by the National Coal Board are allowed up to two months leave with pay which is set off against normal sick pay entitlement.

Several agreements, including those for local authorities services and electricity supply provide for unpaid leave at the discretion of management when the paid maternity leave entitlement has been exhausted and this in effect provides a guarantee of reinstatement in employment.

Generally speaking payment under these various arrangements is conditional on 12 months continuous service at the date of application for maternity leave and sometimes on the understanding that the employee will return to work – if not the employer can ask for a refund.

The private sector

It is not general practice for maternity leave to be granted in the private sector of industry. Some sickness benefit schemes specifically exclude maternity benefit from their provisions, eg the agreement of the Joint Industrial Council for the Cocoa, Chocolate and Sugar Confectionery Industry provides that no payment should be made in respect of absence due to pregnancy.

A survey carried out by the Institute's Information Department in November 1971 found that out of 48 companies only eight had a policy of granting maternity leave and of these, five made no payment. The majority of the participating companies said that no leave of absence was granted and employment was normally terminated 13 weeks before the expected date of confinement when the maternity allowance became available.

Common Market countries

In the EEC little progress appears to have been made in the harmonization of maternity benefits. Of the EEC members, France, Germany, Italy and Luxemburg have ratified ILO convention Number 3 and Italy and Luxemburg only have ratified convention Number 103. Both these conventions which were passed by the ILO in 1919 and 1952 respectively deal with maternity protection. They include provisions for at least 12 weeks maternity leave of which not less than six shall be taken after confinement (additional leave may be taken in cases of medically certified illness); for cash and medical benefits fixed by national laws or regulation to be provided by compulsory social insurance or by means of public funds, and for a woman nursing her child to be allowed time off for this purpose which is to be counted as working hours and remunerated according to agreement. In addition notice of dismissal may not be given during absence on maternity leave.

At one time the European Commission was endeavouring to define uniform measures for the whole of the community on leave and absence for women about to have children, compensation benefits, bans on dismissing women employees during pregnancy etc but it has since decided to abandon this work in view of the development of legislation on the subject in the member states and other difficulties. Nevertheless, the underlying principles of all maternity protection provisions in the EEC countries appear to be the continuance of employment for all purposes during absence through maternity, protection against dismissal, maternity leave, daily breaks and economic security and health protection for working during the period of maternity.

The following outlines the position in France:

(a) No employer can terminate the contract of a female

employee whose pregnancy has been confirmed by a medical certificate. The contract can only be terminated for reasons such as misconduct or where the employer cannot maintain the conditions of the existing contract.

(b) A female employee can suspend her employment for a period commencing six weeks before the presumed date of confinement and ending eight weeks after the actual date. This suspension period can for medical reasons be extended to eight weeks before the date of confinement and up to 12 weeks thereafter.

(c) If the employee decides not to return to work at the end of the suspension period she must inform her employer according to the terms laid down in the contract. The employee may, however, at any time within the year following the expiry of the suspension period request the employer to reinstate her employment and he must then give her priority of employment in his service and in work on which she can use her skills. In the event of re-employment he must grant her all the seniority, pension rights and other status she has acquired at the time she left his service.

(d) After one year's service, hourly paid employees receive 50 per cent of their wages and after two years service 100 per cent of the wages during the absence period of 14 weeks.

(e) After one year's service, salaried employees receive 100 per cent of their salary during the absence period of 14 weeks. For longer service compensation is given in accordance with sickness benefit.*

This statement has been prepared by the Institute's Working Party on Equal Pay and Equal Opportunity. The members of the working party are as follows:

Anne Mackie (Chairman)
Brian Machin
George Mepham
Marjorie Harris
Lady Seear

Bernard Ungerson CBE
Deirdre Rockingham Gill (secretary to the working
    party)
September 1973

---

* Since this Appendix was prepared, Incomes Data have published a
study on maternity leave which adds considerably to the information
given here. *Maternity Leave*, Study No 58, Incomes Data Services,
1973

Equal opportunities for men and women

IPM statement on Government proposals
1 The Institute welcomes the Government's decision to introduce legislation to make unlawful discrimination in employment on the ground of sex.

In previous statements* the Institute has urged the need for such legislation and, at the same time, the repeal of those sections of the Factories Act which class adult women with young persons as needing special attention. It is therefore particularly pleased that the Government proposes to repeal these restrictions (para 1.8 of the consultative document).

Scope
2 While the present proposals constitute a step forward along the path of equal opportunities, they fail totally to tackle the problem of women's rights as a whole. The omission of all matters relating to financial and legal responsibilities, for example, is to be regretted.

3 In particular, the Institute deplores the Government's intention to exclude matters relating to 'retirement, marriage and death'. The Institute is completely opposed

* *Women and Employment*, Policy Statement by the Institute of Personnel Management, September 1973
The House of Lords Select Committee on the Anti-Discrimination (No 2) Bill. Evidence of the Institute of Personnel Management, June 1972

to the proposals as set out in paras 2.7 and 2.8 which will exempt these matters from equal treatment under the proposed Bill and will not require occupational pension schemes to provide benefits for men and women on the same basis.

The 1971 census found that nearly half of all mothers were in jobs and that women were the chief economic supporters of one household in five. These figures would suggest that the Government has not based its plans on the current facts but rather on the traditional view of women's role in society which treats women as mere appendages of men and assumes that a woman's income can never play a significant part in a household.

The Institute would again urge the Government to reconsider its attitude and to stop treating men and women as separate species for retirement and pension purposes (see paras 3.7–3.12 of the IPM policy statement).

Exceptions

4 On the question of exceptions (paras 2.9–2.16 of the consultative document), the Institute feels that these should be very difficult to obtain. For this reason, it is unhappy with the proposed criteria as set out in para 2.11. For example, para 2.11a would provide for a general exception to the Bill "where the nature of the job requires it to be performed by a man". The wording is too vague and could be open to interpretation not on the basis of genuine job requirements but on existing convention and custom. Similarly, 2.11c which refers to forms of social work . . . "where it is necessary to maintain a team including persons of each sex" could give rise to the establishment of dangerous precedents. In particular, a definition of social work is required; otherwise it could be confused with any kind of work involving people, eg personnel management.

The Institute suggests that it might be better to delete

the list of criteria as it stands and to substitute a clause which would require the employer *in each case* to show special and exceptional reasons within the contents of the job why exemption under the proposed law should be allowed.

5 The Institute also objects to the criteria listed in para 2.13. Who is to decide "where it would be offensive to public taste or decency for a man (or woman) to do the job"? One man's decency is another man's prudery. The second criterion, "where it could be shown that for the performance of personal services strong preferences among customers or clients made the employment of a man (or a woman) essential to the business" could also lead to all sorts of abuses. The Government states that it wants to change prejudiced attitudes which give rise to discrimination. It will not achieve this change if it relies on current attitudes as is suggested in this para. The Institute recommends therefore that both 2.13a and 2.13b should be deleted.

6 In para 2.14b, the Institute suggests that the words "a man (or woman)" should be changed to read "men (or women)". Statistical evidence should be derived from a group and not from an individual.

7 There seems to be little real justification for excluding small undertakings (para 2.16). However, if a limit has to be set in the first instance, the Institute recommends that this limit should be set at ten or fewer employees and not 25 as suggested. Furthermore, every effort should be made to eliminate this exclusion as speedily as possible.

Statutory restrictions and protective legislation

8 As previously stated, the Institute supports the Government in its intentions to repeal, in respect of women aged 18 and over, those restrictions in the Factories Act 1961 and associated legislation relating to hours of

employment and to working with moving machinery (para 2.17).

9 However, the Institute can see no good reason to support the argument for retaining the Midwives Act 1951 which confers powers on the Central Midwives Board to issue certificates of enrolment as midwives only to women (para 2.20b). If there are male gynaecologists and obstetricians, why not male midwives? Obviously, a woman should be able to exercise her personal preferences in the matter but the decision not to permit male midwives at all seems illogical.

Enforcement machinery: individuals

10 The Institute accepts that employment cases should first be considered by the Department of Employment's conciliation officers, and then, in the event of failure to reach a settlement, be referred to the Industrial Tribunals (paras 2.21, 2.22, 2.23). It would however point out that Tribunals are concerned only with industry and do not therefore provide suitable enforcement for the other aspects dealt with in the consultative document, eg education. Their use could also create difficulties if the law was eventually extended to include matters relating to women's legal and financial responsibilities.

11 The sentiments expressed in para 2.27 appear to reflect the 'frail female' syndrome. It is suggested that the paragraph should be reworded to read "a man or a woman" throughout. The following sentence might also be added with advantage: "Everything must be done to simplify procedures and the use of the enforcement machinery by individuals".

Discrimination in the professions

12 The Institute considers that professional bodies should not be exempt from the proposed legislation.

Employment agencies

13 Para 2.34 relating to employment agencies should be

strengthened. The Secretary of State for Employment should have powers to *require* the local authority concerned to use its powers under the Employment Agencies Act 1973 to withdraw the agency's licence in cases where an agency was persistently flouting the discrimination laws.

Redundancy Payments Act

14 Para 2.37 proposes to amend the Redundancy Payments Act (and the related provisions of the Contracts of Employment Act 1972) so that, for the purposes of that Act, absence, because of pregnancy would be treated in the same way as absence because of sickness. This would enable a woman who was no longer employed because of pregnancy or sickness to retain her continuity of employment if she began work again with the same employer within 26 weeks. The Institute would further recommend that the employer must inform the employee of her rights under these amendments.

It should be noted that this section leaves unresolved the problem of rights to *reinstatement* on which important matter some policy decision is needed.

Education

15 The Institute agrees with the Government that there is need to take action to ensure that discrimination on the ground of sex does not occur in the field of education. However, it feels that the proposals as set out in this section of the green paper appear weak.

It has been stated that the Secretary of State for Education and Science already has the power to give direction to any educational establishment other than universities if they act unreasonably by discriminating on the ground of sex. But there is little evidence to show that such powers have been used in the past. The Government should therefore take positive action to ensure that these powers are used and if necessary to strengthen the legislation in this area.

16 With reference to para 3.6, the Institute recommends that a study of the extent to which curricula differences and customs contribute to unequal opportunities for boys and girls should be *primarily* the responsibility of the Equal Opportunities Commission with the *assistance* of Her Majesty's Inspectors.

17 The Institute accepts the proposals set out in 3.10 but considers that the reference made in 3.1 to cases of discrimination in employment among teachers in schools should also apply to university staff.

18 Grants for women students should not, in the Institute's view, be influenced by marital status (para 3.11).

The Equal Opportunities Commission

19 The Institute supports the provision for the appointment of an Equal Opportunities Commission with the power to conduct enquiries, to publish its findings and to educate and persuade public opinion (4.2). However, it seems to the Institute that stronger sanctions may prove necessary than those here proposed. At present, there is no provision for a body which would have powers, similar to those of the Race Relations Board, to investigate unlawful conduct where no complaint is made. A body which is intended to persuade and educate such as the proposed Commission may not be appropriate here but progress towards achieving equal opportunities and eliminating discrimination on the ground of sex should be watched carefully with a view to introducing stronger sanctions if these appear necessary.

20 Finally, the Institute would urge that the date of implementation of the proposed legislation should be as soon as possible and certainly *before* the final date of implementation of the Equal Pay Act 1970.

November 1973

2 The role of women in family and society

Chapter 3, on discrimination in education, contains evidence that the development of girls is restricted by the distinction between 'boys' subjects' and 'girls' subjects'. This distinction arises from an assumption about male and female roles. Many women, some with the support of their husbands, have already rejected the view that bringing up a family is their primary role and must therefore determine their needs and activities throughout life. There is now a substantial body of opinion which accepts that young children need not necessarily be in the permanent company of their mothers. Women need no longer be fully occupied in bringing up children, and many with young children now seek work or training for a career to which they can return after a few years.

We have in fact moved away from the situation where the family depended solely on the father as the breadwinner. Increasingly the earning of the family income is seen as a joint task in which, both before and after childbearing, the wife plays an equally important role. Loss of income from either partner is a serious blow to many families. But this change has come about not merely for financial reasons. Although, in the UK at least, the need to raise the family income has been a major driving force, there is growing concern about the waste of human talent that women and the community as a whole have suffered from. Women generally have suffered through the lack of free choice in determining their development and the community has been, and still is, the poorer in consequence.

The present stage in this long process was described in a United Nations (UN) Report in 1970 on the Participation of Women in the Economic and Social Development of their Countries:

" . . . in the vast majority of countries – both developed and developing – women's role is still limited and leaves room for expansion; that there is a general trend towards a more active participation of women in the economic and social life of their countries; and that society is groping for ways and means to cope with this situation and for new patterns to fit the changing roles of men and women.

"Although many replies stated that in principle there was nothing to prevent women from playing a greater part in the economic and social development of their countries, the actual state of affairs shows that there remain substantial obstacles to the attainment of this goal in many countries. While priorities may differ, these obstacles appear to be basically the same, whatever the country's stage of development. They include primarily: lack of proper education and training; lack of vocational guidance and counselling; traditional attitudes of both men and women towards their respective roles in society; the division of the labour market into traditionally 'male' and 'female' sectors; lack of child-care facilities for working mothers, such as nurseries and day-care centres, and lack of labour-saving devices in the home.

"With regard to education and training, it may be noted that in countries where educational facilities are generally inadequate or costly, priority is usually given to boys. Furthermore, in the majority of countries education is geared to the traditional concept of the respective place of boys and girls in society. As from an early age, therefore, a male or female child is conditioned to its future role. Fundamental educational reforms will be required if a change in this basic outlook is to be effected, and if future generations are to be taught that the principle of equality for all citizens means in practice that men and women should have a free and equal choice of

28

occupation, based solely on their individual inclinations, abilities and talents."

The UN Commission (on the status of women) reported that it seemed that the increasing participation of women in economic life had been brought about by the need for greater utilization of the potential labour force, and not by a conscious desire to change the roles of men and women in society. In consequence, the participation of women in economic life is subject to limitations and discrimination. So long as women are seen as a reserve of labour to be called on when needed, we shall all continue to suffer from the frustration of many women and from the waste of their talents.

In its evidence to the Select Committee of the House of Lords, the Confederation of British Industry (CBI) stated that:

"Finally, the frequently marginal value of women's wages and salaries in terms of total family income affects their own attitudes to their own employment."

This statement was, of course, qualified in its submission to the Select Committee and it would be unfair to regard it as a significant part of the CBI's view of the present situation. But the statement was made and it is worthwhile examining the facts to see how relevant it is. There can be no doubt that the contribution of some married women to their families' income is marginal in the sense that their withdrawal from employment would not have disastrous consequences on the family. But the extent to which families generally rely on credit terms to purchase durable consumption goods (or borrow to pay for holidays) is sufficient to make any significant reduction in income a serious matter.

Furthermore, in a significant number of households the breadwinner is a woman. The 1971 Census provided the following information:

Chief economic supporter of households

		Men		Women	
Single	..	12,706		11,445	
Married	..	126,520	⎫	4,349	⎫
Widowed	..	4,859	⎬ 132,739	18,642	⎬ 24,984
Divorced	..	1,360	⎭	1,993	⎭
		145,445		36,429	

(*Source:* Table 29 of Census 1971 Summary Tables

This shows that in 16 per cent of households (20 per cent if single persons are included) a woman is the 'chief economic supporter'. Table 34 of the summary tables shows that in 42 per cent of 'couples' the wife is 'economically active'.

The CBI statement also seems to ignore the fact that a significant number of men earn no more than the majority of women. The Earnings Survey carried out by the Department of Employment in April 1973 showed that 75 per cent of women in full-time employment had gross weekly earnings of less than £28, and that 13 per cent of men also earned less than this amount. (Incidentally, the overlap measured in this way has increased only marginally since September 1968.) Another way of stating the degree of overlap in earnings is that while nearly 11 per cent of full-time male manual workers earned less than £25, in April 1973, 6½ per cent of full-time female manual workers earned more than £25. The overlap is greater in non-manual work taken as a whole. While nearly 18 per cent of full-time men workers earned less than £30, nearly 22 per cent of women on non-manual work earned more than £30. (All of these figures exclude people whose pay was affected by absence.)

The extent to which mothers of young children are in employment is not sufficiently appreciated. The 1971 Census has provided 'activity rates' for women related to the number and age of dependent children:

Percentage of wives and mothers who are economically active

Number of dependent children		Ages of dependent children	
0	43·7%	0–4	20·4%
1	44·3%	5–10	40·6%
2	39·2%	11–15	53·1%
3	35·4%	16 and over	55·2%
4	30·9%		
5 or more	26·3%		
All wives and mothers	41·7%		
All with dependent children	39·7%		

In January 1974 the Department of Employment published projections of the working population to 1986. The projections took into account a further steep rise in the activity rate of married women as follows:

Age	1971	1986
16–19*	42·4	42·4
20–24*	46·7	48·7
25–34	38·4	43·3
35–44	54·5	66·4
45–54	57·0	73·2
55–59	45·5	60·5
60–64	25·2	33·2
65 and over	6·5	9·5

* Includes students as economically active.

Activity rates for both married and unmarried women are set out in Appendix 1. The following warning was given at the end of the article:

"It is recognized that the projected increases in activity rates are subject to the important, over-riding assumption that activity rates for married women will in future follow similar paths through each subsequent age group, as in the post-war period. This, in turn, implies a judgement that economic and

31

social factors will continue to influence increasing percentages of married women to join the labour force.

It is recognized that these judgements are in some sense superficial and that considerable research is needed if the underlying influences are to be fully understood. Some possible factors pointing to changes are the pattern of family building, the availability of child-care facilities, and opportunities for female employment which still show considerable regional variations. It is also apparent that increased activity rates can be achieved only if the economy continues to expand at a rate sufficient to absorb the implied increase in the labour force over the years. One factor is whether increasing opportunities for part-time work can be made available. Another imminent change that may affect activity rate trends is equal pay, although it is not clear in which direction this will influence the trends."

Department of Employment *Gazette*, January 1974

The overall effect of the changes in activity rates on the composition of the working population is shown below:

	1951	1971
Men	68%	64%
Married women	14%	23%
Unmarried women	18%	13%
TOTAL	100%	100%

The percentage of working women that are married had risen from 43 per cent in 1951 to 64 per cent in 1971.

It is evident that the community is already extremely dependent upon married women to maintain, let alone increase, our gross national product, and it seems that this dependence is going to increase.

It is evident, too, that a growing number of families are to a considerable degree dependent upon the mother's earnings. In her study of the economic costs of rearing children and the social and political consequences of these costs, Margaret Wynn has pointed out that the seriousness of the trough in family income that occurs when the wife ives up work to rear children is not dependent upon any absolute standard (a minimum-needs level, for example). The trough is, of course, more serious and lasts longer if the family becomes a large one, or if the period of education is extended (the years added by raising the school leaving age are the most expensive years of dependence). About this period Margaret Wynn has written:

"This coincidence of maximum economic stress in the typical family with the adolescence of the children has many unfortunate consequences. These are the years when children are beginning to think of freedom and independence, and when they begin to see where their own family stands in our competitive society. If relations between parents and children are good then the economic difficulties of the family can be explained to the children who will understand. If relations between parents and children are not so good then the economic stress can be disruptive. Disputes develop between parents and children about money. Adolescents have to learn about money and to experiment with it to form their scales of value. Such experimentation appears to hard-pressed parents to be irresponsible extravagance. Such disputes lead to loss of parental influence and control. If the parents have not built very good relations with their children, the father in particular, in a hard-pressed family, is liable to lose the respect of this teenage children just because of his inadequate earning capacity. Dependent children too often blame the father if they are unable to maintain the standards of their peers.

"The conflict is aggravated by the great contrast between the standard of living of families with children who are still dependent and families with children who go out to earn their living."

Family Policy, pp 148–9

There is therefore a need for a more general and much fuller awareness of the roles that women are playing and will play in our society, and that fuller awareness must have effects on attitudes to the education and training of boys and girls.

In the light of this conclusion, the views allegedly

33

advanced by the then Secretary of State for Education and Science in a letter dated 16 February 1972 seem particularly unhelpful. A representative of the National Joint Committee of Working Women's Organizations informed the Select Committee that, in this letter to the Joint Committee, the Secretary of State had said:

" . . . in her opinion the role of an education service is to reflect rather than to lead society, in that its major task is to prepare its citizens to take their place in it" and "in preparing girls to take their place in society we must keep their likely opportunities and the contemporary social mores very much in mind and this dictates a realistic and pragmatic approach to the problem however altruistic we might be inclined to feel about it."

SBN 401373 pp 65–6

There is, of course, a problem for teachers. They should not be expected to play a leading role in bringing about change – that would be dangerous for society – but neither have they the right to discourage change in attitudes.

The Select Committee received a number of protests about the assumptions often made by those responsible for determining education facilities and for giving career advice to boys and girls. The Select Committee concluded that:

"The crucial importance for the future of the first five years of a child's life is now universally accepted. By that age, observation of the different ways its parents behave, the different sort of toys it may be given, even the pictures in the books it looks at before it can read will have helped the child to absorb an awareness of the roles laid down by our society for the sexes. At infant and junior schools the process will be continued: the games that are played, the interests which are encouraged and the different qualities of character which are approved for boys and for girls, are all subtly conditioning girls to expect and to accept a different, more domestic and often more submissive role in life."

SBN 410473 para 8, p 4

34

Two points that need to be stressed here are first that any observations made today of attributes and interests cannot be accepted as a measure of potential. Children are subjected from birth to influences that to a considerable extent restrict their freedom of choice. 'Conditioning' is not an inappropriate word to describe this process which inhibits so many young people from developing any capacities that are irrelevant to the roles that parents and others have cast for them. The second point is that every aspect of our society (social, economic, technical, political) is changing so rapidly and, for most of us, so unpredictably that we cannot know what talents will be needed by the time our children enter employment.

There is perhaps also a need to keep a watchful eye for the effects on individuals and society of the current trends. Differences of view about the roles of men and women are often genuinely held and should not be ignored. Moral judgements about individual choices here are unlikely to be helpful.

3 Discrimination in education

The Select Committee stated in its report:

"The attitudes of society are reflected in the conditions which the Bill seeks to change and are at the same time formed by those conditions. Women find their employment prospects restricted by their lack of education while they are discouraged from acquiring the necessary qualifications because of limited opportunities outside the traditional sphere of women's occupations."

SBN 410473 para 7

Evidence of discrimination against girls in the facilities and opportunities for education can be extracted from the published statistics. The following examples have been obtained from a study of the statistics. Without doubt there is much more to be said on the matter.

Lack of equal provision (see Appendix 2)

Maintained schools

In boys' grammar schools the provision of courses beyond 'A' level is significantly higher than in girls' and mixed grammar schools: 25 per cent of the boys' schools make such provision, while only 3 per cent of the girls' and 7 per cent of the mixed schools provide them.

Conversely, the provision of courses between 'O' and 'A' level in girls' schools (grammar, technical and comprehensive) is significantly greater than in boys' or mixed schools.

Direct grant grammar schools

The provision of courses in direct grant schools follows a similar pattern but the difference in opportunity to pursue a course beyond 'A' level is even more serious because nearly 40 per cent of the boys' schools make such provision while only 5 per cent of the girls' schools provide them, and there are only two direct grant mixed schools.

Surprisingly, the percentage of boys' grammar schools providing courses between 'O' and 'A' level is higher than that of the maintained boys' grammar schools making such provision (11 per cent compared to 7 per cent).

Independent secondary schools

The provision for girls in these schools is still lower. Only $1\frac{1}{2}$ per cent of the girls' schools provide courses beyond 'A' level compared to $16\frac{1}{2}$ per cent of the boys' schools and only one of the 110 mixed schools. The difference in provision of courses between 'O' and 'A' level is similar to that in maintained grammar schools.

Courses followed (see Appendix 3)

Pursuance of 'A' level courses which include mathematics and science group subjects by boys, in preference to other 'A' level courses, is about as common in comprehensive as in grammar (maintained or direct grant) and technical schools. As one might expect, in secondary modern schools a smaller proportion of boys choose a mathematics/science course in preference to other 'A' level courses.

The percentage of boys that choose to pursue a course including mathematics (but not science subjects) in preference to other 'A' level courses is lower than those referred to above but the pattern between schools is similar.

The percentage of girls pursuing 'A' level courses which include mathematics and science group subjects in preference to other 'A' level courses is lower than the percentage for boys, and the difference is greater still regarding courses including mathematics only. The per-centages in January 1972 were:

Category of School	Percentage on courses including subjects in the mathematics and science group		Percentage on courses which include mathematics	
	Boys	Girls	Boys	Girls
Maintained schools				
Modern	52	20	29	5
Grammar	65	38	48	19
Technical	70	35	54	15
Comprehensive	65	32	43	14
Other	61	30	42	14
Direct grant grammar	61	41	46	22
Independent schools	55	35	35	13

The extent to which girls choose to pursue courses including science subjects and/or mathematics shown by these percentages and the numbers indicated in Appendix 3 may seem surprisingly high in relation to the few opportunities outside teaching that women have for the application of such knowledge in employment.

The percentages leaving school in 1970 with two 'A' levels in science and other subjects were:

	Boys	Girls
Science	46	19
Arts	17	46
Social science/arts	20	20
Other	17	15
TOTAL	100	100

Age on leaving school
Pupils leaving school in 1971 (percentages)

Age*	Boys	Girls
14	29·9	30·7
15	33·6	34·2
16	14·8	15·2
17	14·1	14·5
18 and over	7·6	5·5
	100·0	100·0
(Total numbers	382,300	363,300)

* Age at the beginning of January of the year of leaving
Source: Education Statistics for the UK (1971)

The difference in the age pattern of leaving is very small except for that between the relatively small percentages that stay on to 18 and over (explained no doubt by the difference in provision of courses beyond 'A' level already noted).

There is a difference between the leaving pattern in maintained and independent schools. The position in 1971 was:

Number of 16-year-old pupils as a percentage of pupils three years earlier

	Maintained schools	Independent schools
Boys	33·1	80·8
Girls	32·6	68·0

Source: Evidence presented by the National Union of Students to the Select Committee SBN 401373 p 209

Boys are more likely to have independent school places purchased for them by their parents. In 1970–71 the percentage of boy school leavers coming out of independent schools was 46·7 per cent; the percentage for girls was 37·8 per cent.

Achievement and destination on leaving school
(see Appendices 4 and 5)

The numbers of boys and of girls leaving school with one 'A' level or two 'A' levels are almost identical. The numbers of boys and of girls leaving school with one to four 'O' levels and no 'A' levels are again almost identical. The number of girls leaving school with five or more 'O' levels and no 'A' level is significantly larger than that of boys and the number of boys leaving school with three or more 'A' levels is significantly larger (44 per cent greater) than that of girls.

The percentage of the girls with 'A' levels who go to university is significantly lower than that of boys. Of those with two 'A' levels, the percentage of girls going to university is 11 per cent; that of boys is 21 per cent. Of those with three 'A' levels, the percentage of girls going to university is 58 per cent; that of boys is 68 per cent.

It should be noted that the Monopolies Commission reported that

"In some cases women may find it more difficult to obtain university places for vocational courses and degrees than men of equivalent ability and qualifications."
Report on the Supply of Professional Services, October, 1970

A significant percentage of girls with 'A' levels go to colleges of education. Indeed if entrants to colleges of education are combined with entrants to university, the difference between boys and girls is much reduced. (Of course, the comparison ignores the very much more restricted choice offered to girls.)

Percentage of leavers with two or more 'A' levels going to:

	University	Colleges of education	Total
Boys	52·6%	4·4%	57·0%
Girls	38·7%	22·8%	61·5%

A higher percentage of girls than of boys leaving with 'O' levels only take up full-time further education. This fact, coupled with the higher percentage of girls going to colleges of education, means that a significantly lower percentage of girls than of boys possessing General Certificate of Education (GCE) 'O' levels go straight into employment. How far this difference arises from the relatively lower provision of day release for girls is not known but this could be a factor. One of the consequences for girls is that their delayed entry to employment could help to reduce their opportunities for advancement.

The percentage of all girl leavers going to university or colleges of education is higher than that of boys (except for those from independent schools):

Percentages of leavers going to university or college of education

	Boys	Girls
All maintained	7·0%	8·4%
Maintained grammar	27·8%	30·4%
Direct grant grammar	42·6%	44·9%
Independent	28·4%	21·6%

Achievements at university (see Appendices 6, 7 and 8)

For some years a higher percentage of women than of men holding full value awards from local education authorities has been successful in final examinations. For 1971 the percentages were:

	Men	Women
Successes	84·4	87·6
Premature termination		
Examination failure	6·2	3·2
Other reasons	5·1	6·4
Final examination failure	2·0	1·1
Unknown	2·3	1·7
TOTAL	100·0	100·0

(See Appendix 6)

Thirty per cent of the first degrees awarded in the academic year 1969–70 were awarded to women (a slightly higher figure than the percentage of women undergraduates at that time). The percentage of first degrees awarded with honours was 77 per cent for both men and women taken separately. Eighty-eight per cent of the higher degrees awarded in that year were awarded to men.

The percentage of honours degrees awarded with first class honours was 10 per cent for men and 5·5 per cent for women, but the percentages vary considerably according to subject.

Men form a high proportion (more than twice the number of women) of the total number awarded first degrees in all those subjects where first class honours are relatively more often awarded, to both men and women, ie medicine, dentistry and health; engineering and technology; science; architecture and other professional and vocational subjects. Conversely, more women than men are awarded first degrees in most of those subjects where first class honours are relatively less often awarded, to both men and women, ie education; languages, literature and area studies; arts, other than languages. Exceptions to this pattern are agriculture, forestry and veterinary science, and in the subjects grouped as social, administrative and business studies, where men predominate, but first class honours are relatively less often awarded.

Further education (see Appendices 9 and 10)

Only 10 per cent of girls and women are given day release from employment for further education. The percentage of boys and men given day release is 40 per cent. The difference in percentages given day release is particularly great in electrical engineering (one-twelfth the percentage of males); paper, printing and publishing (one-ninth); timber and furniture (one-sixth); clothing and footwear (one-fifth).

Only a small percentage of girls is provided with sandwich courses (0·8 per cent of those aged 15 to 20 who take some form of further education, and only 0·08 per cent of those aged 21 and over). Only 11 per cent of those taking sandwich courses are girls or women (16 per cent of those aged 15 to 20 and 6 per cent of those aged 21 and over).

Catering and institutional management is the only subject where the number of girls and women on sandwich courses approximates to that of boys and men.

Girls and women make more use of evening classes than the boys and men (particularly after the age of 20). This no doubt reflects the lack of provision for day release.

Girls and women taking 'advanced courses' through evening classes are few relative to boys and men. On degree level courses their numbers approximate to those of boys and men only in education; languages, literature and area studies; and arts. On Higher National Certificate and Higher National Diploma courses their numbers approximate to those of boys and men only in medicine, dentistry and health. On other courses leading to a recognized qualification their numbers approximate to those of boys and men only in education; medicine, dentistry and health and welfare; languages, literature and area studies; arts; and music, drama, art and dancing.

Over the whole field of further education only 2·2 per cent of the female students are taking courses leading to a recognized qualification, compared with 11·1 per cent of males.

In further education courses leading to a recognized qualification, a higher percentage of women than of men holding full value awards from local education authorities are successful in their final examinations. The 1971 percentages were:

	Men	Women
Successes	68·2	72·9
Premature termination		
Examination failure	8·5	3·7
Other reasons	9·4	11·3
Final examination failure	8·4	6·3
Unknown	5·5	5·8
	100·0	100·0

(See Appendix 6)

Summary

(1) A significantly smaller proportion of girls' schools and mixed schools than of boys' schools provides courses going beyond 'A' level.

(2) The almost total absence of direct grant grammar mixed schools increases the disparity in the provision of courses going beyond 'A' level.

(3) The percentage of girls taking courses in science and mathematics is significantly smaller than that of boys. It is said that the continuing shortage of women teachers in these subjects is one of the reasons for the difference here.

(4) The achievements of girls and boys in GCE examinations are about equal up to two 'A' levels, but a much higher percentage of boys than of girls leaves school with three or more 'A' levels.

(5) The difference in age on leaving, between maintained schools and independent schools, is a further factor increasing the difference in opportunity between boys and girls, because a significantly higher percentage of boys than of girls go to independent schools.

(6) A significantly smaller percentage of girls, than of boys, with 'A' levels go to university.

(7) This difference on leaving school is to a degree balanced by the much higher percentage of girls, than of boys, who go to colleges of education.

(8) The percentage of women who fail in first degree examinations at universities is slightly lower than that of men. But a much higher percentage of men get higher degrees. The percentage of first degrees awarded with honours is similar for men and women.

(9) The percentage of honours degrees awarded with first class honours is higher for men than for women (in fact nearly double). It seems that men benefit from the fact that first class honours are more frequently awarded (to both men and women) in those subjects in which they outnumber the women to a considerable

degree. Conversely, women are at a disadvantage in outnumbering the men in subjects where first class honours are less frequently awarded.

(10) The percentage of girls and women given day release for further education is one-quarter of that of boys and men.

(11) Only 11 per cent of those taking sandwich courses are girls or women.

(12) Many more girls and women than men and boys attend evening classes. But relatively few do so for courses leading to a recognized qualification.

(13) Over the whole field of further education 11 per cent of male students and 2 per cent of female students are taking courses leading to a recognized qualification.

(14) The percentage of women who fail in further education examinations providing a recognized qualification is slightly lower than that of men.

In the light of this summary of the present position one can only conclude with the comment that more equal opportunity in employment cannot possibly be achieved without far-reaching changes in our educational system. In the debate about discrimination some proposals have been made. These are considered below.

Nursery schools

It has been argued that since girls develop rather more rapidly than boys in their first few years, the lack of nursery education could be a more serious deprivation for girls. (See, for example, Corinne Hutt, *Males and Females*, (p. 104).

Co-education

Primary schools and establishments for higher education are to all intents and purposes co-educational. At secondary level the proportion of single-sex schools dropped from 48 per cent in 1961 to 40 per cent in 1972.

Most teacher training takes place in mixed colleges. In England and Wales, 86 per cent of teacher training establishments are mixed and the trend is for an increasing number to take both men and women. Except for the single-sex colleges of Oxford and Cambridge, all universities admit men and women.

In its evidence to the Select Committee, the Department of Education and Science drew attention to "a more rapid development in educational standards among girls than among boys; and an increasing tendency towards co-education at both school and university levels". The Department welcomed these trends and considered that they are likely to continue. The Department added that virtually no co-educational establishments were becoming single-sex.

In a report to the 1972 Trades Union Congress Women's Conference, the TUC stated:

> "It is believed that the extension of co-educational schooling where girls and boys are taught together might help girls to appreciate and accept that their own potential ability is no less than that of boys. A further added advantage of co-education would be that girls would then suffer less from the continuing shortage of women teachers of mathematics and science subjects."

> *The Roots of Inequality*, Trade Union Congress

In evidence to the Select Committee a Labour Party Study Group drew attention to the fact that "Differences in curriculum for boys and girls occur even in co-educational schools".

The Select Committee "were not convinced that the evidence showed conclusively that girls' choice of subjects was greatly influenced by co-education". The Committee were however concerned at the discrimination between boys and girls in regard to science and mathematics. They reported that:

> "even for schools built as late as the 1960s the Ministry of Education was recommending a lower standard of science

facilities in girls' and mixed schools. It is lack of opportunity not lack of interest that causes proportionately smaller numbers of girls than of boys to do science and mathematics. There is no evidence to show that girls dislike these subjects ... the idea that 'girls are no good at maths' can easily have a self-fulfilling effect, and inadequate mathematics teaching may very well be a main reason for the still very low number of girls studying economics."

SBN 410473 para 9

The Select Committee also drew attention to the effect of 'timetable administration' in mixed schools on the opportunities for boys and girls. If classes in technical drawing, woodwork and metal work, for example, co-incide with classes in cookery and needlework the segregation is emphasized and therefore contributes to the discrimination throughout life.

The Department of Education and Science stated that legislation to prohibit single-sex schools would require a change in the Education Acts under which any change in the character of a single-sex school in the maintained sector is subject to the approval of the Secretary of State, and the approval could only be given after public notice of the proposed changes, to enable objections to be submitted. Furthermore, legislation against discrimination in schools "would also make it unlawful for those in charge of co-educational institutions to maintain a balance between the sexes".

A Select Committee of the House of Commons considering the Anti-Discrimination Bill accepted these arguments and "the principal of parental choice in education".

Compulsory day release

The National Joint Committee of Working Women's Organizations and the National Union of Teachers have urged that day release should be made compulsory for all young people at work below the age of 18. (Sixth Report from the House of Commons, Expenditure Committee on

The Employment of Women, March 1973.)

The National Joint Committee regretted that the provision for further education laid down in the 1944 Education Act had never been activated. They felt that the disparity between boys and girls in day release was a further indication of the difficulties under which women and girls have to compete for jobs. It could be argued that the introduction of compulsion might lead to a still further restriction in the range of employment open to girls. There would seem to be little point in compulsion if the opportunities for employment of girls were not considerably widened and that is the primary need. An expansion in day release would follow from deliberate measures to widen the opportunities and thus create the need for more training. On the whole, the view of the Department of Education and Science on this matter seems sensible:

" . . . the DES is concerned to see further progress in this matter, and is open to any suggestions which would increase the level of day-release. All the possibilities of doing so on a voluntary basis, by seeking to establish a wider realization on the part of employees and employers of the benefits to be gained from further education, ought to be explored before compulsion is contemplated."

SBN 416072 p 28

It should be noted that the House of Commons Sub-Committee recommended in March 1973 that "the provision of day-release for young workers should be made a statutory requirement on all employers".

SBN 218273 p 25

The Government stated in February 1974 that it was not convinced that compulsion was feasible or desirable and believed that "further progress should be sought on a voluntary basis".

Cmnd 5536 para 34

The pace of change (see Appendices 11 and 12)

Perhaps the most commonly held view is that, while

48

the changes achieved in recent years are welcomed, they have been too slow. Some members of the Select Committee were concerned at what they saw to be a complacent attitude in the Department of Education and Science. The Department's report had drawn attention to the changes achieved in recent years but had made little comment on the differences that remain.

Does the pace of change justify complacency? What are the facts?

The number of girls obtaining GCE 'O' level passes rose by 52 per cent from 1960 to 1970 while the number of passes by boys rose 35 per cent and the total numbers of 'O' level passes by girls is very close to that for boys.

The number of girls obtaining GCE 'A' level passes rose by 168 per cent while the number of passes by boys rose 80 per cent. The numbers of girls and of boys gaining two or more 'A' passes rose 138 per cent and 85 per cent, respectively, between 1961 and 1970. However, the total number of girls leaving school with five or more 'A' level passes remains well below that of boys. The proportion of women undergraduates has grown significantly in recent years.

Number of students on courses leading to a first degree or first diploma (UK)

Year	Men	Women	Total	Women as % of total
1959–60	67,367	22,178	89,545	24·8%
1963–64	76,344	30,244	106,588	28·4%
1967–68	120,105	48,194	168,299	28·7%
1970–71	132,667	57,899	190,566	30·4%

Source: Statistics of Education, 1971 (UK)

The numbers of women entering higher education as a whole has risen since 1961 more than the number of men has (125 per cent as compared to 97 per cent).

A further indication of the rate of progress in higher education is provided by the following trend in qualifications in science and technology:

Persons obtaining degrees or degree level*
qualifications in science and technology
(women as percentage of total)

Subject	1958	1962	1966	1970	1971
Biology	28·8	36·6	40·4	40·3	38·4
Chemistry	13·1	13·0	15·4	16·4	17·2
Mathematics	24·5	27·2	25·0	24·6	25·7
Physics	8·7	8·1	10·9	14·0	13·4
Metallurgy	Nil	2·5	1·3	1·5	3·1

*ie CNAA degree or diploma in technology

Source: The survey of Professional Scientists, 1971, Department of Trade and Industry, HMSO 1973

The percentage of girls and women given day and block release rose from 7·4 per cent in 1962 to 9·6 per cent in 1971 while the percentage for boys and men rose from 30·3 per cent to 35·9, a marginally larger proportionate rise for girls and women but the difference remains very large.

Even if the existing provision for males were no further improved, at least 25 years would pass before the current rate of change brought females within foreseeable reach of equal treatment. Since further improvement for all students will be made necessary by technological and other changes, differences in the opportunities offered to males and females will probably continue for another 100 years or more unless some much more deliberate action is taken to bring about change.

Student grants

The grant for married women students is currently 74 per cent of that for men and single women living at home. Married students, men and women, are entitled to additional grants to cover dependents. Women's organizations have generally expressed resentment at what they regard as quite unwarranted discrimination. The DES says that "Grants are intended to reflect needs after taking account of students' resources", and point out that for single students the grant is in most cases reduced by a parental contribution. The resentment arises from the fact that the married women's grant can only be, and has been, justified by the earning potential of her husband and the assumption that both man and wife should bear the loss of the wife's earnings. Married women generally are contributing to such a significant extent in our economic life that a difference in grant seems no longer reasonable. The resentment has been further strengthened by the fact that the married women's grant has been unchanged since 1971, during which times other grants have been raised on two occasions. The Government has undertaken to examine this matter (*Equal Opportunities for Men and Women*, 1973).

4 Selection for employment and training

Career guidance

" . . . our job as careers officers has two prongs of activity. One is to stimulate people to think of things of which they may not have previously thought. On the other hand, our job is to ensure that their ideas do not become unrealistic . . . one has to recognize that many of our girl clients are already conditioned to restricted ideas about employment before we see them. On the other hand, it is foolish to get carried away with the totally idealistic belief that one must be campaigning in every case for equality if this is only going to lead them into frustration and a general cynicism."

SBN 401373 p 117

In these words a representative of the Institute of Careers Officers (officers of the Youth Employment Service) explained to the Select Committee the difficulties he and his colleagues have to face. They are concerned to play their part in widening the opportunities for girls but are handicapped by the attitudes of employers, parents, teachers and, not least, of the girls themselves who are often reluctant to break outside the limits generally set for them. Even where an employer is willing to engage a girl for an engineering apprenticeship, and there is no opposition from the craftsmen concerned, a good deal of courage is required of the girl to see it through. The choices made are of the greatest importance for everybody concerned and the community has a responsibility to see that the best possible advice is available.

In making a choice, girls need to consider not merely their immediate needs and interests. The probability for most of them today is that both child-rearing and work outside the home will occupy significant periods. The 'return to employment' problem is therefore one with which most will be faced, and it is important that they begin to pay regard to it well before they leave school. The TUC Women's Advisory Committee has expressed the view that "at the present time, careers guidance is seldom regarded as seriously as it should be . . . for girls it is not careers guidance but is primarily occupational guidance and, even as such, it often fails in its purpose". (SBN 218273 p 20)

The House of Commons Expenditure Committee's report includes the following:

> "We regard it as important for school-leavers to see jobs as more than stop-gaps between school and marriage and further that they should be encouraged to take account of a job's prospects. Careers education should include some study of the pattern of woman's working life. The majority of girls still look forward only as far as marriage and do not recognize that they will probably resume employment when their children are no longer completely dependent on them."
>
> SBN 218273 para 5, p 10

One criticism of the present arrangement is that no clear responsibility is laid down. The National Council of Women has urged that the present arrangement, under which the provision of a Youth Employment Service is shared by local education authorities and the Department of Employment, should end and local education authorities should be required to provide a service (SBN 218273 p 104). This requirement has now been placed firmly on local education authorities by Section 8 of the Employment and Training Act 1973.

There has been considerable criticism of the Department of Education and Science's failure to develop an adequate policy on the appointment of careers teachers in schools. The TUC Women's Advisory Committee has said:

> "The numbers of careers teachers need to be substantially increased, with recruits drawn from among teachers with maturity and some years of teaching experience, and with systematic training, organized on an in-service basis. Properly conceived, careers education should be a subject in its own right, calling for specialist teachers devoting their full time to it, in close co-operation with the Youth Employment Service."
>
> SBN 218273 p 20

There can be no doubt that the present provision is totally inadequate and it is to be hoped that a new initiative will arise out of the increased concern that the current debate has stimulated.

In response to a recommendation from the House of Commons Expenditure Committee that "the provision of trained careers teachers should be mandatory in secondary schools", the Government (in February 1974) did not agree that it should depart from the principle that decisions about the employment of particular categories of teachers should be left to the local education authorities and the governing bodies of secondary schools. It also expressed the view that it might be more appropriate to have a group of staff involved in careers guidance, "perhaps linked with a school's pastoral and social arrangements". The then Government also stated that it would be giving 'detailed consideration' to the whole question of training of careers teachers. (Cmnd 5536, paras 17–19)

Discrimination in training

Industrial Training Boards (ITBs) have been heavily criticized for their failure to make any contribution towards widening the opportunities for women.

In 1968 the Association of Teachers in Technical Institutions asked ITBs for information about women covered by their operations. Only three out of 18 boards established before 1967 could tell the Association the number and percentage of women employees being trained. Such data as the ITBs did provide confirmed existing evidence that women are mainly employed in the less skilled and less responsible jobs, and that the range of jobs they do is relatively small in both manual and non-manual fields of work. The small amount of information available about training showed that the percentage of women under training was smaller than that of men. It seems that the ITBs have not considered it to be part of their job to encourage employers to extend the training offered to girls and women. The National Council of Women in its evidence to the Select Committee said:

> "The ITBs will not try and persuade the employers to agree to train women and girls instead of men unless there is a shortage of labour locally. They will improve the quality of training but they will not try and pioneer the training of women for jobs at present always done by men. It is not their function to do so. The Department of Employment has never sent a directive to the boards that they should do so. Nor has the Department of Education and Science made it its business to encourage the training of women and girls as a special priority.
>
> "Another drawback to the training of women and girls is that the ITBs will not try to combat local prejudice, eg the Catering Boards will only train women managers where there is no local prejudice against them. The training of managers and supervisors has increased under the direction of the boards where there is no local prejudice."

SBN 416072 p 124

The Council also expressed concern about the lack of training offered to older women seeking re-entry to employment.

It is therefore a major criticism of Government policy that any improvement in the training provision for women is seen as a matter related to needs of individuals rather than of industry. The need is for better utilization of abilities generally, and an expansion of training programmes could do much towards that objective.

Clause two of the Employment and Training Act 1973 lays a duty on the new Manpower Services Commission to "make such arrangements as it considers appropriate for the purpose of assisting persons to select, train for, obtain and retain employment suitable for their ages and capacities and to obtain suitable employees", and the 'arrangements' *may* include "arrangements for encouraging increases in the opportunities available to women and girls for employment and training". It remains to be seen whether this possibility (it seems it is not a binding obligation) will lead to any new initiative in this matter. It is perhaps significant that an article about the new Commission published in the Department of Employment *Gazette* for December 1973 contains no reference to the subsection of clause two quoted above.

Incidentally, only one of the ten members of the new Commission is a woman and she (the Chairman of the Nottinghamshire County Council) was appointed after consultation with local authority associations in England and Wales.

Under the new legislation the Training Services Agency (taken over from the Department of Employment by the Commission on 1 April 1974) will co-ordinate the activities of the Industrial Training Boards. One of the measures that could be taken to "encourage increases in the opportunities available to women and girls for employment and training" is that exemption from levy should only be given when the Commission (or the Training Services Agency) is satisfied that reasonable opportunities are being offered to girls and women. Consideration should also be given to the House of Commons Expenditure Committee's proposal for "special grants to firms which train girls and women for jobs outside the traditional range of women's work, and to firms which provide training and promotional opportunities for women returning to employment as home-leavers".

Government training centres have made practically no

contribution to the training of women. In September 1972, of 9,700 people in the centres only 33 were women (in December 1970 there were only 20 women). The range of courses offered has been very restricted. Nearly half the places in the centres in February 1972 were in engineering trades, and a further quarter in construction trades.

It seems that the Training Opportunities Scheme has had some effect. By January 1973 4,000 women were in training compared with 1,000 in December 1971, though only 16 were on government training centre courses and the majority of women were at commercial colleges. But these are small improvements in relation to the total problem. Location of the training centres is also reported to be a problem for many of the married women that could benefit from training. Family responsibilities make it extremely difficult for most, and impossible for many, to travel far each day. Part-time training would also help them.

Men and women undergoing courses of industrial rehabilitation receive equal allowances but the allowances for men and women on training courses differ. Men and women aged 20 and over get £12.35 per week and £11.65 per week respectively (October 1973). The House of Commons Expenditure Committee has recommended "as a matter of urgency that this inequality be removed".

The Government pointed out in February 1974 that the differential had been reduced in October 1973 and would be eliminated by the end of 1975 in accordance with the principles of the Equal Pay Act. (Cmnd 5536, para 61). A much higher allowance is paid to a married man of any age but is only paid to a woman if she has an adult dependent. (Currently this allowance is £15.90 for a man, £15.20 for a woman, but this difference will disappear by the end of 1975.) The discrimination here between married men and women workers is parallel to that in student grants (see p 25) and is equally unjustified.

Conclusion

A thorough review of opportunities offered to men and women is called for. Each ITB should, with the help of the Training Services Agency, carry out an examination of the jobs in its industry with the object of listing those jobs where women could be employed (given present legal restrictions) and encouraging, with financial aid if need be, the training of women in jobs for which they are suitable and from which they have until now been excluded. The cooperation of unions must be sought. The women trained under these measures must be given a reasonable guarantee of employment in the jobs for which they will be trained. This can best be assured if the selection and training is carried out within firms. The aim should be steadily to widen the range of jobs open to both men and women.

All ITBs and government training centres should be required to collect and publish data on the sex of trainees and the positions for which they are being trained. Only those firms that give a reasonable degree of cooperation towards this objective should be granted exemption from levy. Exemption should not be granted on the basis of total training effort without regard to the amount of training offered to women.

The Distributive Industry Training Board [DITB] has given a lead in commissioning the Institute of Manpower Studies [IMS] to carry out a manpower survey of the industry. Following pilot surveys, a sample of 2,500 firms of various sizes and types (multiples, retailers, wholesalers) were selected for a survey begun in September 1972. To help the IMS research team, a steering committee with members of the DITB drawn from trades unions and industry as well as the Board's staff, was set up. The broad objectives of the survey were:

(1) to identify the existing manpower resources; what type of people (age, sex, skill), where they are regionally, in what type of business and organization;

58

(2) to measure the movement that is taking place within the industry and between the industry and the outside world; promotion, labour turnover, recruitment etc;
(3) to understand the main factors affecting employment within the industry: what is happening to the way work is organized, what types of business are increasing, and the use made by firms of different forms of training.

The IMS report on the survey will provide the basis for future training policy. The January 1974 Department of Employment *Gazette* contains an article about the survey and highlights some of the findings. While the position of women in this industry is not specifically mentioned, several of the findings concern them particularly and future plans will no doubt be designed to take account of special problems in the employment of women. These findings include:

"the likelihood of increasing numbers of part-time workers in the industry in addition to an existing large 'casual' workforce; the growing concern of firms with employment issues. Over half the firms stated that they had great difficulties with recruitment and labour matters in general;
the extremely small intake of people in the 'trainee' category into firms, and their very high wastage;
the high labour turnover rates generally – especially new recruits in certain occupations. Forty-two per cent of recruits left before completing one year's employment;
the importance to the industry of recruitment direct from school – a feature that will be certainly affected by the raising of the school leaving age."

Discrimination in opportunities for apprenticeship is referred to in chapter 4. Opportunity for training in skilled manual work is necessary if women are to have prospects for better pay levels, but it is also important as a foundation for training and development for non-manual careers (draughtsmen and technicians).

The employment services
When the House of Commons was debating reports of

the Expenditure Committee, and in particular that from the then Employment and Social Services Sub-Committee, Robin Chichester-Clark, Minister of State for Employment, emphasized the important part of the job centre programme in achieving the Government's aim "to have manpower services which concentrate on helping people choose and get particular jobs and helping employers to get the right people quickly". By 1980 there would be 8,000 job centres, better located than the present exchanges, better staffed to provide an employment service and providing a more appropriate atmosphere. Unemployment benefit would be managed and organized separately. The subcommittee received much evidence from interested organizations and individuals. The following points were amongst the issues raised in evidence.

Some members of staff in the exchanges have an inadequate knowledge of the needs and qualifications of those seeking work. In particular, the mature married woman seeking to return to the labour market has special needs to which too little attention has been paid.

Vacancy display and the self-selection scheme is proving attractive to both employers and employees. It helps to overcome the dole image. The Department of Employment reported that "there has been no sign that many people try to get jobs for which they lack the necessary qualifications or experience". The time spent on routine interviewing has been cut, so that staff have more time to give advice to those who have special difficulties. The intention is to provide self-service facilities in all new offices and every office will display as many vacancies as possible.

The TUC and several other organizations urged that notification of vacancies should be compulsory. When compulsion was introduced in 1952 it was hoped that this would help the Ministry to steer people to areas where there was an acute shortage of labour. The compulsion was generally regarded as a failure and was withdrawn in 1955.

Today, the need is more to help the unemployed to find work. The TUC thought that compulsion could help. The Association of Officers of the Ministry of Labour felt that it would be better to attract custom from employers by giving satisfaction in filling vacancies. The sub-committee attached weight to the argument that as the processing and sorting of information in the exchange was computerized, compulsion to notify all vacancies could be introduced without many extra staff.

The sub-committee recommendations included:

> "That officers with specialist knowledge of the matters most closely affecting women at work should be available to give advice in job centres.
>
> "That as soon as employment exchanges are in a position to accept and process the information there should be a statutory requirement to notify all vacancies to the State employment offices."

SBN 218273 pp 25–26

In February 1974 the Government considered these recommendations and expressed the view that "the much improved training of employment advisers at present being introduced would enable them to provide the standard of counselling service envisaged by the Committee". (Cmnd 5536, para 76)

The Government believed that compulsory notification of vacancies was not the best way to ensure that the service had a bigger role in the labour market. It believed that the improvements in the service being made would gain the confidence and full cooperation of employers. (Cmnd 5536, para 77)

5 Discrimination in employment

The facts about the numbers of men and of women employed in different occupations have been widely publicized in recent years and attention is repeatedly drawn to evidence which shows that there has been little if any change over the years in the proportion of women employed in most occupations. There are only men in some occupations and very few women in some others. Few women get into positions of high responsibility in any field and, with some notable exceptions, they are few in professionally qualified employment. There is even some evidence that the number of women in some senior positions has declined in the past 30 years.

These facts are not in themselves conclusive evidence of discrimination as defined in the introduction, ie "treatment of an individual, on grounds of sex, less favourably than other individuals". But the facts taken as a whole and the significant differences in opportunities for women in different fields of employment can leave no room for doubt that discrimination against women is general.

The Select Committee of the House of Lords heard evidence and examined witnesses over a period of nine months, and reported that:

"After hearing the evidence some members of the Committee concluded that the problem of discrimination on the ground of sex went deeper than they had originally thought. The virtual absence of women among the upper reaches of employment suggests either that there is a bias against the employment of women, or that there are few women qualified to be appointed. In either case the situation is unsatisfactory."

SBN 410473 para 89

What then are the facts? To what extent do the opportunities for women differ from one field of employment to another? What are the main causes of unequal opportunity?

The Civil Service (see Appendix 13)

The Civil Service (non-industrial) has for many years been regarded as a leader in providing more equal opportunities for women. The position in January 1972 in the Administration Group was as follows:

Number of women as percentage of total employed
Administration Group

Grade	Total employed*	Women as percentage
Under Secretary and above	499	2·8
Assistant Secretary	1,046·5	5·3
Senior Principal	403·5	1·5
Principal	3,184·5	7·5
Senior Executive Officer	4,553	6·0
Higher Executive Officer (A)	99	22·2
Higher Executive Officer	13,239	14·3
Administration Trainee	287	31·4
Executive Officer and Higher Clerical Officer	35,984·5	27·8
Clerical Officer	84,762	55·0
Clerical Assistant	65,441·5	76·5
All grades	209,000·5	52·6

*Part-time employees counted as halves

Source: SBN 416072†
†In Appendix 13 the position in some Departmental Executive grades is shown

In its report on the employment of women in the Civil

Service, a Departmental Committee pointed out that present proportions of women were not a true reflection of their current opportunity to enter the Service. The Committee reported that:

"In the last few years, women have been an increasing proportion of entrants to the Assistant Principal grade and there has been little significant difference between the performances of men and of women in the competition for assistant principal. Almost half of those now successful for entry to the executive officer grade are women . . . "

Civil Service Department Management Study No 3, June 1971

The tables on page 65 are taken from this report.

In its evidence to the Select Committee, the Civil Service Department reported on the numbers of men and women entering the Administrative Group during 1971:

Numbers of women entering the Administration Group as percentage of the total entering

Grade	%
Principal	12·5
Administration Trainee	37·4
Executive Officer	44·5
Clerical Officer	57·2
Clerical Assistant	73·3
Total	66·6

Comparison of the present grade percentages (see Appendix 13) with those entering the higher grades shows that the opportunities for women have improved at the point of entry. However, opportunities will remain unequal until women have improved opportunities for promotion and changes are made in working arrangements to facilitate the employment of women with family responsibilities.

The Civil Service Department reported that:

"Promotion procedure . . . is the same for men and women and they have equal opportunity to obtain promotion. Neverthe-

Open competition for entry to the Assistant Principal grade

Successes and entrants as percentage of applications from each sex

	1968		1969		1970	
	Successes	Entrants	Successes	Entrants	Successes	Entrants
Men	12·3	6·9	8·7	5·1	9·1	4·6
Women	8·3	5·0	7·4	3·7	8·0	6·6
Total	11·0	6·3	8·3	4·7	8·7	5·3

Note: Year relates to year of competition and not necessarily to year of actual entry.

Source: Civil Service Commission.

Open competition for entry to Executive Officer grade and equivalent departmental grades

Successful applications

Year	Men	Women	Total	Percentage of total who are women
1963	944	634	1,578	40·2
1964	1,083	677	1,760	38·5
1965	1,506	1,071	2,577	41·6
1966	2,020	1,441	3,461	41·6
1967	2,378	1,579	3,957	39·9
1968	1,137	950	2,087	45·5
1969	1,834	1,526	3,360	45·4
1970	2,632	2,170	4,802	45·2

Source: Civil Service Commission

less, in each group or class in the Service women are concentrated in the lower grades. One of the main causes of this is the greater turnover of women, many of whom leave, mainly to get married, before they have served long enough to achieve promotion . . . the only objective evidence of women doing significantly worse than men in promotion was in the junior executive grades". (In the higher grades the numbers and proportions are so small that promotion rates are said not to be reliable guides.)   SBN 416072 p 66

The Departmental Committee reported that the figures could be seen as evidence of bias against women but that statistics alone are not proof of discrimination. Departments had some evidence that more women than men refuse promotion because of mobility problems or domestic commitments. The Committee recommended that, because prejudice may remain in the Service, particularly where women have not traditionally worked, "appointments should be solely on the grounds of suitability and qualifications" and that "departments should arrange for promotion boards to consist of both men and women". The Committee's other recommendations to facilitate the employment of women are considered in chapter 6.

The law

On 5 August 1971 the Attorney General gave the following figures in response to a question:

	Men	*Women*
High Court Judges	70	1
Official Referees	3	0
County Court Judges	114	1
Full-time Chairmen and Deputy Chairmen of Quarter Sessions	22	1
Queen's Counsel in Practice (approx.)	300	2
Recorders	92	1
Stipendary Magistrates	48	1
High Court Masters and Registrars	44	1
County Court Registrars	120	0
Lay Magistrates at 1 January 1971	12,550	6,700

The Select Committee of the House of Lords found that:

"In the legal profession women often have difficulty in becoming articled to solicitors, and encounter even greater problems in obtaining interesting work once they are qualified. Those who wish to become barristers often find their sex a disadvantage when seeking places as pupils or tenants in Chambers – in 1972 of 2,714 barristers only 167 were women."

SBN 410473 para 76

Population census reports show that the number of women classified as judges, barristers, advocates and solicitors rose from 1,290 in 1961 to 1,700 in 1971 and, as a percentage of the total number so classified, from 3·9 per cent to 4·3 per cent. In the Civil Service, 11 per cent of legal appointments were held by women in 1971.

Accountancy

The president of the Institute of Chartered Accountants stated recently (*Guardian*, 9 11 73) that 1·6 per cent of the Institute's members are women. In the mid-1960s only 1·1 per cent were women (*Equality for Women*, M Rendel). The population census reports show that the number of women classified as accountants, company secretaries and registrars rose from 13,660 in 1961 to 21,900 in 1971 and, as a percentage of the total numbers so classified, from 13 per cent to 17 per cent.

Universities

In July 1972 the following figures were given in response to a question in the House:

	Men	Women
Vice-Chancellors	44	nil
Heads of University Departments, Institutes and Schools of Education	42	nil
University Registrars	44	nil
Principals of Colleges of Agriculture	44	nil
Principals of Polytechnics	28	nil
Principals of Medical Schools	23	1
Members of the University Grants Committee	19	2

In June 1971 only 44 out of 3,281 university professors were women and half of these were in London University. Eleven per cent of the 32,161 full-time teachers at universities throughout Great Britain at the beginning of 1970 were women. (The census data in Appendix 14 shows 13·5 per cent.)

Doctors and dentists

In its evidence to the Select Committee of the House of Lords, the Department of Health and Social Security stated:

> "There are no discriminatory arrangements for the employment of doctors or dentists in the National Health Service, and no fields of work which are barred to women or exclusively to women."

The position in 1970 was:

Women as percentage of total

All hospital medical staff	14·0%
All dentistry staff	8·5%
General practitioners – doctors	12·2%
,, ,, dentists	7·3%

The dental service relies heavily on dental hygienists to clean and polish teeth and on dental auxiliaries to do simple fillings and extractions. All dental auxiliaries and the great majority of dental hygienists are at present women. Both are advertised as careers for girls.

The Select Committee reported that auxiliaries are employed only in public health services, and commented:

> "Perhaps because they are women, perhaps because dentists fear professional competition, they are not widely used."

The Department of Health and Social Security drew the Select Committee's attention to its efforts to enable doctors with domestic responsibilities to continue practising. "It is estimated that almost 20 per cent of all women doctors in the UK are not working, 50 per cent work part-time and only 30 per cent full-time." (Select Committee

Report, SBN 410473, para 52)

The Select Committee received many complaints alleging discrimination by the medical schools, and heard evidence from the Deans of the major schools. Allegations of 'quota systems' were generally denied and, where higher qualifications had been required of girls than of boys, it was said that the practice had been stopped. Since the medical schools are autonomous bodies, the Select Committee sent an enquiry to all of them, and the replies showed that four schools (Dundee and Liverpool Universities, Charing Cross Hospital and St Mary's Hospital) operate a definite quota of women. Women account for about one-third of the total number of students in all the schools and one-third of the applicants are women. Dissatisfaction of women students is said to arise from the lack of part-time post-basic training.

None of the schools admitted to requiring a higher academic standard of women candidates, but several pointed out that in practice the women selected tend to have higher 'A' levels; this could be due to the pressure on medical school places but possibly also because past experience had shown that women who are subsequently shown to be of comparable ability to men achieve higher 'A' levels than the men candidates.

The Select Committee reported:

> "All the medical schools who wrote to the Committee made the point that women spend less time in medical practice than to men. All the schools who limit the number of admissions of women claimed that they did so because they consider it their duty to provide a sufficient number of doctors for the NHS."

SBN 410473 para 21

It was reported in February 1974 that, in a letter to the Secretary of State for Education and Science, the Committee of Vice Chancellors and Principals of the UK universities had affirmed its opposition to discrimination against women entrants to medical schools and had advised universities to abandon any quota arrangements. At the same time the Committee expressed concern about the higher rate of wastage that would inevitably follow any significant increase in the percentage of women entrants and urged the Government to obtain an early and careful study of this problem.

Nurses

Entry into the nursing profession is open to both men and women and there has been equal pay for many years. Women continue to fill most of the positions in nursing the physically ill but the position is different in the mental hospitals. The position in September 1971 was:

	Total no. of nurses	Women as percentage of total
Non-psychiatric hospitals*	227,958	95%
Mental illness hospitals	40,342	64%
Mental handicap hospitals	19,765	66%

* ie acute chronic and specialized
Source: SBN 416072 p 36

The Department of Health and Social Security informed the Select Committee that:

"It is customary in a general hospital for women patients in the main to be nursed only by women",

and added the comment:

"The present practice . . . seems reasonable. There is no doubt that a substantial proportion of women patients would object to being nursed by men. . . . There is no indication that this limitation poses any obstacle to the career prospects of male nurses."

SBN 416072 p 36

The evident assumption that men are incapable of sympathy and giving tender care, and that women are incapable of exerting physical restraint, is surely not supportable.

The Select Committee reported that several witnesses had drawn attention to the fact that, even in this established women's profession, senior appointments for women are becoming fewer. As hospitals grow, increasing numbers of men are being appointed as chief nursing officers, replacing the traditional matrons.

Midwives

This is one of the small number of occupations that is, by law, restricted to one sex. The Midwives Act 1951 empowers the Central Midwives Board to issue certificates of enrolment only to women. The Act makes it an offence for a man, other than a qualified medical practitioner, to attend a woman in childbirth, except under the direction and personal supervision of a qualified medical practitioner. The Royal College of Midwives has opposed any change in the law on the grounds that a man cannot adequately fulfil the 'psychologically supportive' aspects of the midwife's role, and the Central Midwives Board "considers that public opinion would be against such a change". In giving evidence to the Select Committee on behalf of the Department of Health and Social Security, H C Salter, Under Secretary, said "we think the public may not yet be prepared to have men as midwives".

Men cannot obtain the Health Visitor's Certificate because they are barred from midwifery. The Secretary of State and the Council for the Education and Training of Health Visitors have agreed that entry to this profession (ie health visitor) should be open to men and women.

Other medical appointments

Medical auxiliary professions such as occupational therapists, radio-, physio- and speech-therapists have very few men. The Select Committee commented that they "are poorly paid".

Ancillary jobs have, under an agreement with the staff, been divided into a man's and a woman's schedule.

These schedules will be combined as a result of an agreement to introduce equal pay by December 1975. Employing authorities will then be free to engage men or women for any of these jobs, providing they are capable of performing the duties required.

In its evidence to the Select Committee, the Department of Health and Social Security made the comment:

> "From a practical point of view, however, notwithstanding equal pay, it is not thought that the mere amalgamation of schedules is likely to change quickly the employing authorities' preference for employing men on jobs requiring greater physical strength or of an unpleasant nature; or of employing women on those requiring manual dexterity or perhaps service."

SBN 416072 p 47

Teachers and education administrators (see Appendices 15 to 22 inclusive)

Some general statistics for 1970–71 are:

The public sector

77% of teachers in primary schools were women

43% of teachers in secondary schools were women

39% of teachers in secondary schools were graduates and 63% of these graduates were men

54% of the non-graduates in secondary schools were men

Assisted and public sector

58% of teachers in special schools were women

48% of teachers in assisted grammar schools were women

34% of teachers in colleges of education were women (but they include only 25% of the positions filled by graduates)

15% of teachers in establishments for further education were women

(14% of graduates, 16% of others)

53% of all teaching positions were filled by women

(36% of those filled by graduates and 60% of those filled by non-graduates)

Married women

Nearly half the women in primary schools and nearly a quarter of those in secondary schools are married. (More detailed figures are given in Appendix 15.)

The Select Committee received much evidence about the teaching profession and found that:

"Women are in a majority in the teaching profession and there is a policy of equality in appointment and promotion. Any allegation of discrimination is investigated. There are special courses to induce former women teachers to return to the profession. Despite these policies, while the overall ratio of men to women is 42 to 58 in maintained schools, in the lowest graded posts (ie assistants) it is 24 to 76, and in the highest (ie head teachers) 60 to 40. . . . This imbalance of women in senior positions is usually attributed to the fact that women do not apply for promotion but this was contradicted by several women, who told the Committee of their unsuccessful attempts to obtain senior posts.

"The Department of Education and Science 'would not like to say' whether there is a trend to replace headmistresses by headmasters, as was alleged by several witnesses. It is not denied that men tend to be appointed to headships of mixed schools. . . . With the increase in the number of large co-educational schools the number of women's headships are steadily declining. In January 1971, there were 994 mixed comprehensive schools, of which only 53 had women heads."

SBN 410473 paras 65 and 66

The General Secretary of the National Union of Teachers stated recently that the number of women headmistresses has declined by 2,000 since 1965 (when equal pay was achieved). (*Guardian* 9 11 73). Some further statistics are given in the appendices and the following conclusions can be drawn from them:

Appendix 16

As one might expect, the proportion of women head teachers and deputy heads in maintained primary schools is higher than that in secondary schools.

In maintained secondary schools, the grammar schools seem to provide better opportunities for promotion for women than do others, presumably because there are as many girls' grammar schools as there are boys' (separate figures for these are not given in the *Statistics of Education*).

The rank order of maintained secondary schools in terms of the percentages of posts held by women is as follows:

Head teachers	Deputy heads	Second masters and mistresses	Dept. heads	Scale 3 posts	Scale 2 posts	Scale 1 osts
G	G	⎧M	G	G	G	G
M	⎰M	⎰C	M	⎰M	⎰C	⎰C
⎰T	⎱C	⎱G	C	⎱C	⎱M	⎱M
⎱C	T	T	T	T	T	T

G = grammar M = modern C = comprehensive T = technical

The prospects for women graduates is marginally better than for women teachers as a whole, particularly in grammar and technical schools.

Appendix 17

The proportion of senior posts in further education held by women is considerably below that in secondary schools. Trained women have a better chance of promotion than untrained women.

Appendix 22

Nearly half the principals and deputy principals (at 31 March 1971) in colleges of education were women. This is very surprising. The proportion of women teachers in those establishments is about 34 per cent.

Appendices 18 to 22 inclusive

In these appendices the numbers of men and women teachers with qualifications are shown. From these figures the following summary has been made:

Numbers of full-time women teachers with university degree in mathematics and science as percentage of total numbers with these degrees, (at 31 March 1971)

Schools/colleges	Maths	Science	Reference to appendix
Maintained			
Primary	48%†	40%*	} 28
Secondary	31%†	19%*	
Direct grant grammar	42%	36%‡	19
Independent			
Primary	17%	24%	} 20
Secondary	20%	18%	
Primary secondary	44%	38%	
Further education	10%	7%	21
Colleges of education	23%	22%	22

* Based on those with physics or chemistry as first subject

† Based on those with mathematics as first subject

‡ Includes medicine, technology and agriculture

From the table, it can be seen that education provides significantly better opportunities for women mathematics or science graduates than any other field of employment.

Management in industry and commerce (see Appendices 14 and 23)

Statistics on the numbers employed in management positions vary according to the definitions employed. For example, from the figures set out in Appendix 14 derived from the census report for 1961, 1966 and 1971, it would appear that 3·1 per cent of the management positions in the engineering industry and allied trades are filled by women, but the Department of Employment statistics in Appendix 23 for these industries show only 2·3 per cent of such positions (including works superintendent and departmental managers) are held by women. The Department of Employment data is likely to be more in accord with the definition accepted in industry and it is therefore probable that the other census percentages of women in industrial management are also on the high side.

The Select Committee heard a great deal of evidence about the widely held view that women are temperamentally unsuitable for management positions. For example:

"This (ie management in industry and commerce) above all is the area of discrimination. They (girls) are reckoned to lack the right masculine qualities for management whether of sales departments, branches of banks, insurance companies or building societies. The masculine quality most often quoted is dealing with other men. A predominantly male atmosphere (which is virtually a club) can exist at management level: only the ablest and most confident women can penetrate it."

Institute of Careers Officers, SBN 401373 p 115

"The way the world is organized at present . . . requires a number of skills which are very variegated and very complex. There is no reason to believe that men *en bloc* are more endowed with these skills than women. For example, the function of a board of directors of a large organization requires a series of skills in human relations, judgement, intuitive perception of situations, grasp of trends in world situations and so on. There is no reason to believe that men have more of these than women."

Dr R Rapaport representing a Political and Economic Planning [PEP] Research Group SBN 416072 p 62

"Even in areas where, by agreement, men and women can be employed on equal terms, it has sometimes been found impracticable for management to promote a woman to a supervisory post since, where men predominate, they often refuse to work under a woman supervisor."

Civil Service Department, SBN 416072 p 70

It is evident that there is a vicious circle here. Few women apply for management training or senior posts, either because they have accepted the general assumption about women's unsuitability for managerial roles, or because they see little point in trying to knock down 'the brick wall of prejudice'. The Select Committee concluded that:

"Because so few women are taken on as management trainees or gain experience in lower or middle management, they are not equipped to tackle the higher level posts for which, by innate ability and temperament, they may be suited. As a result, women tend to be in support roles . . ."

SBN 410473 para 79

Personnel management is one of the 'support roles' that used to offer a particularly attractive career to women. But as the function became an integral part of management, women steadily lost ground to men. According to Mary Niven two-thirds of the IPM membership were men in 1957 and three-quarters in 1961 (*Personnel Management 1913–63*, IPM 1967).

The Institute's 1970 salary survey showed the degree to which women are concentrated in the lower level posts:

Number of women as percentage of the total at each level

Specialist posts	Percentage	Total numbers
Senior specialist manager	nil	30
Specialist manager	6·5	201
Senior specialist officer	8·9	393
Specialist officer	20·4	426
General posts		
Senior personnel manager	2·2	179
Personnel manager	6·7	584
Senior personnel officer	14·5	476
Personnel officer	27·2	379

A survey (carried out by the author) in mid-1973, covering 36 companies, showed that, of the 1,737 staff in the personnel function that were 'qualified' (as defined for the survey), only 219 were women. The survey provided data on the career and salary prospects currently being offered to men and women respectively. The differences in median salaries by age were:

Age	Median for women as percentage of median for men
25	80
30	81
35	78
40	75
45	71
50	68
55	66

These percentages reflect both the differences in opportunities for advancement and the lower salaries paid to women.

The Institute analysed the advertisements published in its monthly journal, *Personnel Management*, during 1971 and found that 46·9 per cent specified 'male only required', 8·5 per cent specified 'female only required' and the remaining 44·6 per cent made no such specification. In 67 per cent of the senior jobs advertised only males were invited to apply and none were 'female only' appointments.

Scientists, technologists, engineers and technicians (see appendices 15 and 23

The census reports (see Appendix 14) show that in 1971 9 per cent of chemists, physical and biological scientists were women, and that this was higher than the percentage in 1961 (7 per cent). The number of women engineers was very small and only 0·7 per cent of the total, but here again the position had improved since 1961 when it was 0·2 per cent. The proportion of women technologists, technical and related workers rose from 2·6 per cent in 1961 and 5·7 per cent in 1971. The number of women laboratory assistants and technicians, the lowest level classified in the technical area, was 38·8 per cent in 1971 and 32·3 per cent in 1961.

The Department of Employment data summarized in Appendix 23 shows a different picture for the engineering and allied industries. Women scientists and technicians make up only 1·2 per cent of the total in that category in May 1972 and there had been a fall from 1·8 per cent since May 1969. Women 'other technicians' were 2·3 per cent of the total; here again there had been a fall (from 3·4 per cent in May 1966).

In the Civil Service the position on 1 January 1972 was as follows:

Number of women as percentage of total in each grade

Science group	Total number	%
Deputy Chief Scientific Officer	209·5	nil
Senior Principal Scientific Officer	641·5	0·8
Principal Scientific Officer	2,056·5	2·0
Senior Scientific Officer	3,769·5	4·7
Higher Scientific Officer	3,303	6·3
Scientific Officer	3,256	15·9
Assistant Scientific Officer	4,158	29·5
All Grades	17,394	12·5
Technology group		
Directing Grade	157	0·6
Superintending Grade	405	0·5
Principal Professional and Technology Officer	1,704	0·5
Prof and Tech Officer Grade I	3,328	0·7
Prof and Tech Officer Grade II	7,118	0·3
Prof and Tech Officer Grade III	10,438·5	0·5
Prof and Tech Officer Grade IV	13,703·5	0·6
All grades	36,854	0·5

(Part-time staff counted as halves)

Source: SBN 416072 p 7

In March 1971 the five institutes within the Council of Science and Technology Institutes carried out a survey among their members. Although the response was, on average, only 65 per cent, and the results may therefore not be entirely representative, some interesting data was obtained. From the published tables, the following data has been extracted:

Analysis by Institute

Institute	Women	Men
Institute of Biology	528	2,690
Royal Institute of Chemistry	380	13,081
Institute of Mathematics and its Applications	187	1,445
Institution of Metallurgists	26	3,603
Institute of Physics	212	6,216
Total	1,333	27,035

Analysis by Type of Work

Type of Work	Women	Men
General Management	12	2,365
Research and Development	441	11,203
Other Scientific and Technical	247	6,167
Education	584	6,415
Other	49	885
Total	1,333	27,035

Analysis by Age Group (Percentages)

Age Group	Women	Men
Under 25	24·2	7·1
25–29	25·8	19·5
30–34	11·7	17·5
35–39	9·2	15·3
40–44	10·1	14·5
45–49	7·2	10·4
50–54	5·9	6·8
55–59	4·7	5·8
60–64	1·1	2·5
65 and over	0·1	0·5

Analysis by Employer (percentages)

Employer	Women	Men
Central Government and Armed Forces	10·5	9·4
Hospital Board	2·9	1·1
Local Authority (including Colleges and Schools)	35·1	15·9
Nationalized Industry or Public Corporation	4·4	6·9
U.K. Atomic Energy Authority	0·9	2·9
University	12·8	11·0
Industrial or commercial company or private firm	26·3	48·6
Consulting practice	0·6	0·6
Other employers	6·2	2·6
Self-employed	0·5	0·9

In Appendix 31 an analysis of income by age group is given. The overall median incomes were £1,980 per annum for women and £2,830 for men.

In Appendix 31 an analysis of income by age group is given. The overall median incomes were £1,980 per annum for women and £2,830 per annum for men.

In the light of these figures it is surprising that in its evidence to the Select Committee, the Institute of Careers Officers (the professional body for officers of the Youth Employment Service) said, of positions at technician level, "This is perhaps the one of least prejudice". It is true, as they said, that "opportunities for girls with better than average ability and limited ambition do exist, particularly in laboratories". But there are no grounds for complacency or satisfaction about the opportunities for promotion in private industry or the Civil Service. The lack of opportunity in this field is in fact a reflection of, and at the same time a cause of, the lack of education and training opportunities already noted.

Draughtsmen

The Select Committee made considerable efforts to obtain a satisfactory explanation of the fact that only 1 per cent of draughtsmen are women. They had heard that in Sweden 50 per cent are women. In spite of the acute shortage of draughtsmen in the 1960s, few employers seem to have considered the employment of women, giving as a reason the long period of training required. It is a sad fact that, with the decline in the demand for draughtsmen in the past few years, the proportion of women has fallen still lower. In the engineering and allied industries, which employ three-quarters of draughtsmen in manufacturing industry, the proportion fell from 1·5 per cent in May 1966 to 0·9 per cent in May 1972 (see Appendix 23). Indeed, over this period the number of draughtswomen was halved. The position in the Civil Service is evidently better. At 1 January 1971, 11 per cent of those in the draughtsmen class were women. The Draughtsmen's Union has always publicly opposed discrimination and has actively supported demands for equal pay. It surely should have been possible to make progress in this occupation. The decline in the number of draughtswomen is a good indication of the obstacles to progress in industry.

Journalists and broadcasting

In May 1972 the National Union of Journalists carried out a survey with the object of obtaining the facts about discrimination against women journalists, who number 4,500, ie 17 per cent of the total journalist members. The survey showed that only 38 women were holding senior posts for which men would also have been considered, ie editor or chief reporter, and another 18 held jobs for which men would not often have been considered (eg women's page editor, knitting editor).

In evidence to the Select Committee, representatives of the Women in Media Group quoted the following figures from a survey in June 1972 covering 2,000 journalists, of whom 200 were women:

	Men	Women
Reporters	635	92
News sub-editors	409	11
Feature writers	199	29
Woman's page editors	11	50
Sports writers	278	1
Photographers	239	2
Executives	235	11

Source: SBN 410473 para, 87

The representatives also quoted the following figures provided by the British Broadcasting Corporation (in mid-1972):

Position	Men	Women
Current Affairs		
Directors	7	nil
Producers	32	3
Personal assistants	15	3
Researchers	6	14
School Programmes		
Producers and assistant producers	15	10
Personal assistants	5	2
Researchers	equal numbers	
Arts Features		
Producers and assistant producers	26	4
Researchers	4	3
Science Features		
Editors	4	nil
Producers	15	nil
Personal assistants	10	nil
Researchers	13	3
Light Entertainment		
Producers/directors	17	1
Personal assistants	13	nil

	Men	Women
Film Department		
Film editor	9	nil
Assistant editor	61	nil
Assistant film editor	80	9
Lighting	40	nil
Cameramen	46	nil
Assistant cameramen	62	nil
	9	nil

Source: SBN 416072 p 112

In May 1973 the BBC made a public declaration of its intention to see that "in future women will be given a positive opportunity of demonstrating whether they can carry out their duties satisfactorily in areas which appear suitable to their talents and qualifications but where up to now they have seldom, if ever, been appointed" (*Financial Times*, 11 5 73). In future no vacancy would be advertised for men only and selection would depend on qualifications and merit. Progress would be reviewed after 12 months. The Select Committee came to the conclusion that "discrimination in this area ('The Media') was rampant". SBN 410473 para 85

The church

In the Anglican, Roman Catholic and Orthodox churches, women are barred from consecration as bishops or ordination as priests, although there is no bar to the ordination of women in many of the nonconformist churches. Discrimination is also present in faiths other than Christian. The population census reports show that the percentage of women among those classified as clergy, ministers of religion and members of religious orders, declined from 23·6 per cent in 1961 to 16·8 per cent in 1971.

In his evidence to the Select Committee, His Grace the Lord Archbishop of Canterbury said:

" . . . the ordination of women is a matter which should be considered afresh, but the Church of England itself should do

84

this."

SBN 416072 p 139

The Select Committee reported:

> "In all the circumstances it seemed to the Committee appropriate that the Act should not apply to priests or ministers of any denomination, nor to their training or education. This exemption should not, of course, apply to religious bodies in relation to their lay employees."

SBN 410473 para 103 (a)

Service on public bodies

Without exception, the organizations representative of women, and some others too, made strong protest in evidence to the Select Committee at the under-representation of women on public bodies. In consequence, a wealth of information on this matter has been gathered together. In his evidence to the Select Committee, Edward Bishop, MP, quoted the following:

> On 49 public boards of a commercial character, including the Electricity Council and Electricity Boards, the Gas Council and Gas Boards, the Post Office and British Rail, there were in January 1972 422 men and five women.
>
> In the 12 months ending August 1972, 129 appointments or re-appointments to these Boards were made; only one was a woman (and she was re-appointed).
>
> On the 12 Area Gas Consultative Councils there are 84 women out of a total membership of 328.
>
> On the 12 Area Electricity Consultative Councils there are 46 women out of a total membership of 322.

SBN 416072 p 187

A representative of a Labour Party study group that presented a comprehensive report to the Select Committee stated that in October 1972, of 256 members of the eight English Regional Planning Councils, only 13 were women.

The National Council of Women has urged that legislation should be designed to overcome discrimination in these appointments. "Discrimination tends to be indivisible." The lack of opportunity for women to participate in public bodies restricts their development for responsible positions in industry and commerce. Equally, of course, the limited opportunities for promotion to responsible positions must restrict the contribution they can make to public affairs generally. The pressures for and against change here are strong and change will no doubt be slow in the meantime. The Labour Party study group's recommendation that the criteria for appointments to public boards should be broadened to take greater account of the consumer interest, which women can well represent, is surely sensible.

Officers in trade unions

In view of the strong resentment against the lack of women on public bodies, it is sad to note that few women play an active part in their trade unions. In the National Union of Journalists, for example, where 25 per cent of the members are women, and 25 per cent of those holding office in chapels or branches are women, in 1972 there was only one woman among the 30 members of the Executive Council and she was the third of four elected since the union was founded in 1907. In most unions, the extent to which women hold office at any level is small by comparison with the NUJ. One example quoted to the Select Committee by a TUC representative is that there was no woman on the delegation from the National Union of Teachers at the 1971 Congress.

To what extent this is due to a greater lack of interest amongst women members than men, or to a general acceptance that the unions are a 'man's responsibility', is a matter of opinion. Domestic responsibilities must, of course, be a considerable handicap for many married women.

Opportunities in manual work (see Appendices 23 and 24)

The data set out in the lower half of the table in Appendix 23 shows that little change in the employment of women on manual work in the engineering and allied

86

ndustries has occurred since 1966. The small percentage of supervising jobs performed by women rose from 4·4 per cent to 6·1 per cent (there was a 50 per cent rise in the number of women supervisors in electrical engineering). But the even smaller percentages on skilled work fell (from 2 per cent to 1·5 per cent in production and from 0·9 per cent to 0·5 per cent in maintenance). The number of women recorded as 'inspectors and markers off' fell by a fifth (by one-third in vehicle building) and the number of women classified as welders fell by a half (but was doubled in vehicle building).

It is unfortunate that this series of statistics is now confined to engineering but it seems unlikely that any more significant changes will have occurred in other manufacturing industries. In 1968 29 per cent of the employees in manufacturing industries as a whole were women, 5 per cent of skilled production workers were women, 1 per cent of skilled maintenance workers, 45 per cent of other production workers and 13 per cent of foremen and chargehands. The industries that made the best use of the manual skill and experience of their women employees were clothing, footwear, textiles and pottery. The engineering and allied industries have, it seems, not improved their relative position since then.

The general structure of employment

Examination of the data set out in the Appendices, and of the information, views and experience quoted in this chapter, leads to the following conclusions:
1 The opportunities for qualified women workers to achieve promotion in all fields are poor relative to those of men. They are undoubtedly best in teaching, although men may be gaining ground here as large mixed schools become more common. Opportunities are relatively good in the medical and social welfare services, although appointments are restricted generally to 'support' services. Opportunities for qualified women in industry and commerce are generally

inferior to those in the public service, but in most specialist professions the opportunities in the Civil Service are not as good as seems to be generally supposed. The opportunities for women scientists in the Civil Service are no better than in industry. The same can be said about women accountants.

2 The segregation of 'men's jobs', and 'women's jobs' continues, because of the traditional reasons and assumptions about male/female capacities or interests.

3 Only a small proportion of women obtain training for the most skilled manual jobs in industry and supervisory positions are generally held by men.

4 The analysis of type of employment entered by school leavers shown in Appendix 24 shows that the greatest difference is in the proportion of boys and girls going into apprenticeships leading to a skilled occupation. Hairdressing and manicuring is the only apprenticeship open to girls in significant numbers.

5 Both girls and boys have few opportunities for employment leading to a professional qualification. As we have seen in chapter 3, more boys than girls obtain qualifications before entering employment. In manufacturing industries as a whole (but not in engineering and allied industries) the percentage of girls entering employment where 'planned training' is provided is higher than that for boys. In several industries this factor could offset a little the inequality arising from the lack of apprenticeship.

6 It is as well to be reminded that neither men nor women are very satisfied with their present opportunities in employment. Dissatisfaction arises from a number of factors, as is shown by the report on the General Household Survey carried out in 1971 (see Appendix 25).

The causes of unequal opportunity

There are probably no occupations where a single factor can be pointed to as the major cause of discrimination. Amongst the most significant causes are the following:

1 Inadequate awareness of the roles that women are playing in society and of the harmful effects of unequal opportunity, coupled with a stubborn insistence that women's proper place is in the home (see chapter 2).

2 Unequal opportunities for education and training. False assumptions about adult roles and about male and female aptitudes and interests are major factors here (see chapters 3 and 4).

3 Prejudice against women, often arising from untested assumptions about differences in ability to assume responsibility and cope with role relationship problems in business, politics (see chapter 5).

4 Fear that jobs, and indeed vital tasks, will not be carried out because not enough women remain in, or return to, employment. This fear must be coupled with the fact that, in most fields of employment, little if anything has been done to facilitate the retention and re-entry of married women (see chapters 5 and 6).

5 The cost of higher absence that is unavoidable for most women with family responsibilities.

6 Maintenance of the traditional segregation of work into 'men's' and 'women's'. The cost of training is certainly a significant factor making it difficult to breach this division.

7 Personal preferences, or assumptions about such preferences, eg with regard to nurses and midwives.

8 The 'provision' of some auxiliary posts, eg in medicine and dentistry, and even teaching, has no doubt satisfied to a degree the demand for wider opportunities. Low pay ensures that few men seek to enter these occupations.

9 The 'vicious circle': few candidates, therefore few vacancies offered, therefore few trained, therefore, few candidates . . .

10 Finally, the fact that women in general, have been less ready than men to join trade unions must have had some bearing on male attitudes. General statistics can be very misleading. When men and women work side by side on similar jobs and in comparable proportions, union

membership has become as much a matter of course for women as for men, and no doubt the overall figures are much influenced by relatively weak organization in occupations where women predominate. Nevertheless, the weakness of trade union organization amongst women has, no doubt, been an added reason for men in occupations where there are few women at present to resist any attempt to open the door to them.

The overall position is that, while the percentage of men in the working population that are in unions has remained at about 50 per cent (48·4 in 1961, 53·5 in 1972), the percentage of women in unions has risen from 24 per cent in 1971 to 33 per cent in 1972. But the increase in women membership over this period was about 400,000 while male membership rose by 500,000.

6 Changes needed to facilitate the employment of women

Discrimination between the sexes derives from adherence to traditional differences in perceived roles. In Chapter 2 evidence is presented which shows that many men and women have rejected the view that child-bearing is the only important role of women. An increasing number of women are seeking a career outside the home and resent the restricted choice offered to them. The great need is for a more general and much fuller awareness of the roles that women are playing today.

It is absurd to go on regarding women as a reserve of labour to be called on when needed. They are as essential as men for our economy. Our standard of living could not be maintained, let alone raised, if married women did not return to employment after child-rearing. Measures designed to facilitate the employment of women should therefore be seen as essential for the community as a whole and not merely as costly benefits given away under pressure.

Such measures can usefully be divided into three groups:
(1) Those that will make the working situation more appropriate for women with family responsibilities (eg hours of work, arrangement of holidays, special leave, nurseries).
(2) Those that will reduce as far as possible the differences in treatment of men and women as economically active

91

members of the community (eg taxation, social insurance, retirement, pensions, sick pay).

(3) Those that will ensure the best use of talents, qualifications and experience (these have been discussed in other chapters).

In April 1970 a Departmental Committee was set up to

"consider the employment of women in the non-industrial Home Civil Service; and in particular to examine

a how far women might be given more part-time employment in positions of responsibility;

b how it might be made easier for a married woman to combine looking after a family with a Civil Service career; and

c what retraining might be given to make it easier for women to return to Civil Service employment after a lengthy period of absence."

The Committee's report was published in October 1971 (Civil Service Department, Management Study No 3, *The Employment of Women in the Civil Service*). The Committee's recommendations, which are set out in Appendix 26), were accepted in principle by the Government, and some have been implemented following consultation with the National Staff Side. The Committee recommended that within two years a review of progress should be carried out.

The report of the House of Commons' Expenditure Committee, referred to in previous chapters, also contains recommendations that are relevant here. These are set out in Appendix 27 and will be referred to under the appropriate headings.

Hours of work

Part-time employment

The Department of Employment *Gazette* for November 1973 contains an article which shows the extent to which the number of women taking up part-time work is increasing. In manufacturing industry the percentage of women employees working for not more than 30 hours per week increased from about 12 per cent in 1950 to about 20 per cent in 1972. The percentage for all fields of employment has risen from about 25 per cent in 1961 to about 32 per cent in 1972.

Industries with the highest percentages on part-time are agriculture, forestry and fishing; distributive trades and professional and scientific services with about 40 per cent, and miscellaneous services with about 48 per cent. In public administration and defence about 25 per cent of women are on part-time.

The most recent data on the occupations of part-time employees is obtainable from the *New Earnings Survey* for April 1972, and this showed that, of the 21,000 part-time women in the sample, 42 per cent were in catering, domestic and service occupations; 10 per cent in professional and technical occupations and 17 per cent in office and communications. The New Earnings Survey also showed that 28 per cent of part-time women worked 16 hours or less, and a further 30 per cent worked over 16 but not more than 21 hours.

The Department of Employment has summed up the position: most part-time women employees are "over 35, married, with small families". As the National Board for Prices and Incomes reported in 1971, "The main reason why women worked part-time (rather than full-time) was family commitments". (Report No 169, *General Problems of Low Pay*).

Clearly part-time work is a significant feature of employment. It is evident that part-time employment is more easily found in unskilled and semi-skilled manual work than in the occupations where substantial periods of training are required, and is almost non-existent where the level of responsibility is high. The Civil Service Departmental Committee had this to say about the general problem of part-time employment in higher grade posts:

"Several major departments, at our request, carried out a preliminary survey of the kinds of work at all levels which, if management difficulties could be overcome, could be done on a part-time basis. The survey indicated that there was a wide variety of such work throughout the classes and grades, though there were problems associated with its organization and management. In the administration grades some departments thought that only research type work, where little contact with others was needed, was possible; others that the work of some principals, for example, could be reduced or divided to provide, with some reorganization, part-time posts. The difficulty in providing part-time work in higher administration posts is that in many the work must be under the control of one officer because it calls for consistency in the exercise of judgement on the questions arising and the officer concerned must be available throughout the working day. Nor can management work at any level, or supervisory work, easily be done on a part-time basis. But there are many areas of work where these difficulties do not arise. Departments suggested that in the specialist and professional areas there is scope for more part-time posts for (among others) doctors, lawyers, scientists, economists, statisticians, librarians, and inspectors of various kinds. . . .

"In addition to the benefits of retaining and re-engaging experienced civil servants, there are advantages for management in offering part-time posts. At present it is, generally, only in the last resort where not enough full-time staff, or only full-time staff of very poor ability can be obtained, that departments now consider recruiting part-time workers. It is sometimes suggested that part-time workers are inefficient or debase the standard of the grade: but where part-time workers have been engaged some departments have found that the standard of their work is higher than that of the full-timers. Where the work can be organized to provide part-time jobs, the general level of efficiency of the staff can therefore be raised. A similar raising of standards can be achieved by creating part-time posts for routine work, for example, at clerical assistant levels where, as some departments have already found, routine work tends to be done better for a shorter working day. . . .

"But it is not easy to reorganize Civil Service work to provide part-time posts. It has generally been organized on the assumption that staff, mainly men, work full-time, and any major change from this pattern to account for the different career patterns of working mothers will create problems, not only of management and accommodation, which need time to be resolved. Nevertheless we consider that there are good reasons why the Civil Service should now endeavour to provide more part-time posts for the substantial number of women who are recruited to the Service at all levels, have been trained and acquired valuable experience, but who cannot work full-time in the Service because of family responsibilities. In brief these reasons are: to ensure that the training and abilities of these women are not lost to the Service; to give such women the opportunity of making the best use of the skills which they have acquired; that experienced and able part-time workers can be of great value to departments in certain types of work at times of temporary pressure or shortage of staff; and that certain jobs are done more efficiently by people working part-time.

(Hence recommendation No 10 in Appendix 26)

The House of Commons Expenditure Committee reported that:

"A further disincentive to the employer in providing part-time work results from the protective legislation which limits employment of women to certain hours. As female nurses are not required to desert their hospitals at some arbitrary hour of the night, we consider that it is ridiculous to prevent other female employees from working through the night. We can see no valid reason for this antiquated system to continue".

SBN 218273 para 24, p 19

Flexible working hours

The current debate about the pros and cons of flexible working hours has to a considerable degree been linked with the demand from women's organizations for more accommodation to the needs of working mothers in particular. Civil Service policy, for several years, has been to encourage flexible hours where this can help to spread the level of rush hour traffic, and the Departmental Committee concluded that there would appear to be more scope for management to arrange hours of work to suit staff needs.

There seems to be a general feeling in manufacturing industry that the scope for flexible working hours, if it is not to lead to serious losses in efficiency, may be limited. The number of employees covered by arrangements that have attracted attention so far is not great. The need at this stage is for more controlled experiments, and there is sufficient evidence of net advantages for both employer and employees to give grounds for confidence that there are areas of work where experiments would be worthwhile. One advantage of flexible working hours is that the system enables women to cope with unexpected domestic crises. It must have advantages for both employer and employee over part-time work in some situations. An advantage in any situation is that it provides an opportunity (often much needed) for building trust and confidence into the employer/ employee relationship.

The demand for part-time work and for flexibile working hours needs to be seen against the present background of facilities for working mothers. There can be little doubt that more adequate provision of facilities (notably pre-school nurseries and play centres outside school hours and during holidays) would make full-time (or longer part-time) work a practicable proposition for more working mothers, many of whom are in great need to earn more than they get at present.

Part-time conditions of employment

Incomes Data Services' *Study of Part-time Work* (No 62, October 1973) has drawn attention to the inferior conditions of employment under which part-timers are generally employed. Those who work less than 21 hours a week have no protection against unfair dismissal, no entitlement to redundancy pay, nor is there a minimum period of notice laid down for them; they have no legal right to a written contract of employment. Part-time employees often have no opportunity to join a pension scheme, they get no holiday pay and rather more part-time workers than full-time are not covered for sickness absence by company schemes (see table on p 88). On the other hand, in some cases an enhanced rate is paid to part-timers. Evening shift manual workers in engineering, for example, get a premium of one-fifth (though a good many people in the industry regard this as an anomaly). Still, when there is an enhancement of rate it does help the part-time worker to meet the cost of transport out of a relatively small wage packet. The IDS study showed that in general part-time women workers are on lower average hourly earnings than full-time women workers.

In addition to these disadvantages, most part-time employees have little prospect of advancement, though this is probably not reckoned to be much loss so far as the majority of employees on unskilled and semi-skilled work are concerned.

Holidays and special leave

The main issues considered by the Departmental Committee under these headings concern:

(1) Provision for married women to take annual leave at the same time as their husbands
(2) Unpaid leave for school holidays
(3) Extended unpaid leave for mothers after long service
(4) Unpaid leave to enable a Department to retain the services of an employee whose husband has to move his employment
(5) Paid maternity leave.

Not much comment on the first two matters seems called for. They are common problems where wives and mothers are employed and employers generally have learnt to cope with them in a reasonable way. But they do add to the costs of employing married women and will undoubtedly continue to be a handicap to women's employment. There is a growing demand for the provision of play centres during school holidays. In some large urban areas, local authorities provide centres during holidays and after school hours. The Expenditure Committee came to the conclusion that:

> "There is a need for comprehensive and widespread facilities for the under fives and a particular need for special facilities to cover awkward hours and provide centres for school age children during their holidays. A much more realistic approach is needed if the problems of working mothers during school holidays are to be met. Play leadership schemes in schools and parks as well as the use of school and other premises during the day, with facilities available for providing meals during school holidays for children whose mothers are at work are ideas which should be actively pursued by the Secretary of State for Social Services."

SBN 218273 para 23, p 18

Extended periods of unpaid absence are generally not practicable except perhaps for lower-grade work, because any guarantee of re-employment would be unfair to the person who fills the gap. Furthermore, where high-grade responsibilities are involved, absence of several years would often see changes in other personnel and in organization that would make re-entry a considerable problem for everybody concerned. One can only hope that it will become more commonly accepted that the careers of both wife and husband are of importance to them and that some effort is made to weigh up the impact of moving house on both partners (as well as on the children's education). The Civil Service seems to have provided a fair degree of lattitude here: The Civil Service Department informed the Select Committee that:

> "Departments may also grant unpaid leave for a period normally not exceeding three years to a man or woman civil servant whose spouse is required, for employment reasons, to

move to a place where the wife's or husband's employment in the Civil Service cannot be continued. Unpaid leave of between six and 12 months, at a time to be agreed with the department, may also be granted to women who have children and who have had at least 20 years' service. This arrangement also applies to any civil servant with 20 years' service who has borne heavy domestic responsibilities for a long period in addition to their Civil Service career. The Service also recognizes the difficulties of staff who have elderly or infirm parents or relatives and, amongst other assistance, provides for unpaid leave to be granted for periods appropriate to the circumstances."

SBN 416072 p 68

Maternity leave

In the Civil Service both established and temporary staff are eligible for two months' paid leave for confinement, and unpaid leave within limits according to status and service can be granted in addition. On medical advice, the Departmental Committee decided that the paid leave should be extended to three months (for established staff). The third month's pay would depend on three months' effective service being given on return. The paid leave counts against sick leave. A normal limit of six months' total leave is applied. The Committee's recommendations have been implemented.

An Income Data Services Study (No 58, August 1973) showed that:

"The most striking difference between the UK and other parts of Europe is that, here, the law does not protect the women's employment in any way during pregnancy, and the employer is under no obligation to keep her job open after confinement. In most of the countries (surveyed) there is legislation guaranteeing maternity leave, protection against dismissal, and in some cases the right to re-instatement for up to a year after childbirth." (The comments concerning 'special leave' are, of course, also relevant to this situation.)

Outside the public sector, protection is rarely found in the UK. The European Economic Community countries provide 'generous' state maternity allowances too, and in some the employer is obliged to give maternity pay for a period.

The 1971 census (1 per cent sample tables) showed that, of the three million wives and mothers with dependent children under five years of age, about 600,000 were in employment. The social problem with which we are faced here is certainly not a minor one. The figures quoted below in regard to the provision of nurseries show that a considerable number of mothers returns to employment within months of childbirth.

Dismissal on grounds of pregnancy may be judged fair by an Industrial Tribunal. In a recent case a mother of two was refused discretionary maternity leave by London Transport and dismissed when she refused to resign. The Tribunal decided that dismissal was not unfair because the employee's young and growing family would need greater attention, claiming even more of her time. Another consideration was that her sickness record was a poor one, including 'unexplained absences'. London Transport's medical officer had advised the woman against continuing in employment. London Transport managers have discretion to grant maternity leave and, for the particular manager concerned, this was only the second time in ten years that he had refused maternity leave.

Finally, perhaps one should emphasize the need to counsel mothers and particularly those expecting their first child. Human concern and consideration must surely be particularly important for the expectant mother. The Council for the One-Parent Family (previously the National Council for the Unmarried Mother and her Child) drew the Select Committee's attention to the inhuman treatment still occasionally accorded to girls and women who become pregnant outside marriage. Often their main need is to obtain relevant advice and information; employers have some responsibility, and indeed some interest too, to see that they know where to get it.

As part of its proposals for legislation concerning

equal opportunity, the Government intends to amend the Redundancy Payments Act so that, for the purposes of that Act, absence due to pregnancy would be treated in the same way as absence due to sickness, and a woman absent because of pregnancy or sickness would retain her continuity of employment if she began work again with the same employer within 26 weeks.

Nurseries

In its evidence to the House of Commons Sub-Committee (SBN 218273 p 171) the Department of Health and Social Security [DHSS] reported on the day care provided for 'priority' children (principally those with only one parent who has no option but to go to work). In March 1972, 466 local authority day nurseries provided places for 22,574 children; 853 registered private nurseries provided places for 23,000 children, and 24,331 registered child minders looked after 55,334 children. The Sub-Committee reported that it had been estimated that the unmet need for full- or part-day care for 'priority' children alone was some 85,000 and that the total unmet need must be considerably greater.

Charges are on the basis of actual cost including meals etc plus "a fair proportion of central administration costs". However, the Department say that the means of the persons concerned should be taken into account.

The Council for the One-Patient Family reported to the Sub-Committee that 35 per cent of day nurseries are in the London area or in the counties adjacent to London (but the Kent County Council provides none!). Present plans for urban development seem to be totally inadequate.

Some hospitals provide day nurseries. The DHSS reported in June 1972 that there were 77 in England and Wales and that these were used by about 2,000 staff. A few of them gave priority to or restricted the use to nursing staff. In the main the nurseries were set up and are run without voluntary help. Despite the need to maintain a

24 hour service and complicated staffing schedules, 35 per cent of all nurses are married. (SBN 401373 p 198)

The Civil Service Departmental Committee recognized that the cost of providing nurseries (a subsidy was thought to be inevitable) could be higher than could be justified by the Service as an employer. The Committee felt that doubts could be resolved by an experiment, and accordingly recommended that at least one nursery be set up for an experimental period of four years outside London. Fees would be related to salary, with a maximum based on economic cost.

Few companies provide nurseries for employees' children and it is extremely unlikely that many more would give serious consideration to the matter.

A trade union view on the matter was put to the Sub-Committee by representatives of the National Joint Committee of Working Women's Organizations. They would prefer nurseries to be provided by local authorities. They saw this as a community responsibility rather than a company one.

The Council for the One-Parent Family, on the other hand, has welcomed industrial nurseries, provided the standards and quality of care are controlled and fees are on a nationally agreed basis.

The Sub-Committee reported:

"We consider that it is important that pre-school facilities should be universally available. Until this stage has been reached we welcome any contribution that industry itself may feel able to make towards the provision of such facilities though we would not wish in any way to encourage the Departments of Health and Social Security and of Education to shelve their ultimate responsibility for the provision of day-care and nursery school facilities for all who require them. Further, we recommend the rapid expansion of day nurseries and nursery school provision with flexible hours adjusted to the requirements of working mothers, and in particular, we support the establishment of nursery centres under the supervision of the Department of Education and Science."

SBN 218273, para 22, p 18

In February 1974 the Government commented on the Sub-Committee's recommendations (see Appendix 27) on this matter. This comment showed how little the needs of working mothers had been recognized. After stating that there was no prospect of a rapid expansion of day nurseries, and referring to plans for a 'special building programme' to expand nursery school provision, the Government stated:

> "The object of the new policy is to promote the educational development of the child, but it will also considerably lighten the workload of mothers, by affording them a few hours respite each day from the tasks of child care. Some mothers may be able if they wish to take the opportunity to go out to work on a part-time basis."

Cmnd 5536, para 69

The Government was evidently not aware of the great number of mothers who were already at work and in desperate need of proper facilities for their children.

Home work

The present inadequate provision of nurseries and play centres has induced many women to seek work that can be done at home. Although home work is supposed to be registered by local authorities, the extent of home work is not known and in practice little is registered. The trade unions generally are concerned at what they see as severe exploitation. The Sub-Committee recommended that the Department of Employment:

> "undertake an enquiry into the conditions under which home work is carried out, to obtain reliable figures on the evasion of registration, and to ensure that this registration is properly enforced in the future."

SBN 218273, para 33 p 23

In February 1974, the Government pointed out that there was no statutory requirement to register premises where home work is carried on but, under the Factories Act

1961, employers of home workers in 'many classes of work' are required to keep lists of such workers and supply copies to the local authority. Factory Inspectors had been reminded of the need to see that this requirement is met.

The Safety and Health at Work Bill 1973 contained proposals covering home workers. The then Government indicated that it was still considering what purposes could be served by an inquiry and how it might best be undertaken (Cmnd 5536 paras 80–84).

Absenteeism

There is growing evidence that the sweeping generalization about high absence of women is grossly unfair; the overlap in absence records of men and women is considerable. The record of many men is no better than that of many women, and the extremes of high and low for men and women are similar. There is also no doubt that the level of absence is related to the level of responsibility involved in the work.

Some relevant statistics are set out in Appendices 28 and 29. These are extracted from the recently published report on *The General Household Survey* which was carried out in 1971. The first of these shows that the most common reason for absence was holidays. The youngest group was the least likely to have been on holiday at the time the sample was taken (due to their shorter holiday entitlements). Ill-health was the other major reason for absence and, although the absence of younger women (ie aged 18 to 34), was higher than that of men in this age group, the reverse was found for older groups. Absence for 'personal and other reasons' was found to be more common among women than men, and the difference was particularly marked in the 25 to 34 age group (as one would expect).

Overall, the difference in absence between men and women is thus particularly significant in the 18 to 34 age group. The second of these Appendices shows that women's absence tended to be shorter than men's. The median for women was less than one week, while that for men was between one and two weeks. Absences for 'personal or other reasons' were mostly less than one week.

In deciding to employ a large number of women, employers must reckon that some of them will be unable to attend as regularly as most employers have come to expect of employees in general. This has become so much a fact of life that it is common practice on production lines to legislate for a relatively high level of unpredictable absence by employing spare operators to fill gaps in the line. The cost is considerable and has certainly been one of the reasons why some employers have been worried about the added cost of equal pay. Indeed, some women employees have also become anxious about their prospects for continued employment with the introduction of equal pay. In its evidence to the Sub-Committee, the Union of Shop Distributive and Allied Workers said:

> "while society expects many women to have two jobs, one paid employment and the other her domestic commitments and yet does not expect the same degree of family responsibility from men, then specific provision should be made to lessen the burden on these working women by making provision to cover domestic calls upon them."

SBN 218273 p 120

Consideration should perhaps therefore be given to offering a less demanding contract, where the work permits, to men and women who feel unable to give a guarantee of attendance at the normal level. In return for acceptance by the employer of the added cost of unpredictable and relatively high absence, the employee would have somewhat reduced benefits: for example, the sick pay entitlement might be shorter and the holiday entitlement lower.

This approach to the related problems of costs for the employer and of demands on the employee would, in my view, be more appropriate and less harmful than that proposed by USDAW:

> "A code of sound practices in the field of employment of

women, prepared by the Department of Employment and issued with the authority of Parliament might be another way of expressing parliamentary concern and support in a positive manner. Such a standard-setting guide for employers could be an important stimulus to changes in attitudes and practices."

SBN 218273 p 120

Such a code would, quite unnecessarily, help to maintain the segregation of men and women in employment. Unnecessarily because for many women, in most firms a majority, special treatment is not called for and if the facilities referred to above were more generally provided, more married women would find it possible to reduce their level of absence.

It has been suggested that the offer of less demanding contracts would create a second class of employee. It could, of course, be seen in that light, but it is just as likely that many women would see it as a welcome opportunity to take employment (even full-time) without the normal pressures. It should not be forgotten that some men also have family commitments and dependents and often find these difficult to meet because of pressures on them as employees. For these reasons, it would be necessary to consider carefully the areas of work where such a contract could be offered without serious consequences for overall performance, and eventually to review the situation in areas where it was being used.

The second group of measures are those that will reduce as far as possible the differences in treatment between men and women as economically active members of the community. These include various aspects of social insurance, contributions and benefits, taxation, retirement and pensions, sick pay.

Social insurance

Our present social security system is still in essentials based on the Beveridge Report, and the justification for the discrimination between men and women was the assump-

tion that married women are dependents and could therefore only be entitled to most benefits on the basis of their
husbands' insurance. This assumption about the status and
role of women in the family and society was, it is now
increasingly thought, questionable even in 1940. It is
certainly not a valid one today (see chapter 2). Beveridge
assumed that married women would not normally be in
employment. We know now how events have upset that
assumption. Revision of the system to take account of the
change in the role of women is long overdue. The inequalities with which we are concerned are many and the
whole matter is extremely complex. Inequalities which
affect most women are:

1 The married woman in work who pays a contribution
  receives sickness and unemployment benefit at a lower
  rate than a single woman. She is free to make no contribution (except a small one for industrial injury) and
  would then receive no sickness or unemployment
  benefits. A married woman who pays a contribution can
  qualify for the higher rate of benefit if either:
     (i) "she is living with her husband who either receives
     a retirement pension, an invalidity pension or an
     unemployability supplement or is otherwise incapable
     of self support," or
     (ii) "she is living permanently apart from her husband
     and he is paying less towards her support then the
     difference between the standard weekly rate for mar-
     ried women and the higher weekly rate for single
     women." (See National Insurance leaflet 12 p 21)
  Most married women opt to pay only the small contribution to cover industrial injury insurance.
2 The single woman pays a lower contribution than a man.
  Her sickness and unemployment benefits are the same as
  a man's. If she does not continue contributions after
  marriage, she has to re-establish her right to sickness and
  unemployment benefits when she re-enters employment.

107

Credits for contributions can be obtained, subject to certain requirements, for any period for which a maternity allowance is paid.

There seems no justification for the retention of these differences. Men and women in employment should contribute and receive benefits on the same basis and on the same scale. The married woman in work should be required to pay the full contribution and should receive full benefits. It should probably follow from this that, when a man falls sick or is unemployed, he should receive no additional benefit for his wife if she is employed. In a recent comment on the Government's Consultative Document, *Equal Opportunities for Men and Women*, the TUC argued that opting out by married women should be discontinued but suggested that women returning to employment shortly before retirement (say 50 or over) might continue to have the right to opt out.

The position of married women not in employment also needs to be reviewed. They are not covered by social insurance at all, and if they fall ill the plight of the family has to be carried by the family without assistance (unless they have privately insured against this possibility). A study group of the Labour Party put forward to the Select Committee the suggestion that:

Married women engaged on domestic duties at home and not in paid work would (under our proposals) in general remain liable for the payment of flat rate contributions (at the same rate as a man). These would provide insurance cover for chronic sickness (but not short-term illness) and incapacitating disablement, and for ultimate retirement pension. Married women with children under school-leaving age staying at home to look after the family would however be credited with flat-rate contributions until the youngest child passed school-leaving age. The contributions credited to women ensure the benefits outlined above (for chronic sickness and incapacitating disability) and also entitlement to unemployment benefit without waiting period on re-entry into the field of employ-

108

ment when the children reach school-leaving age.

SBN 401373 p 25

The study group put their proposal as part of a general change in the status and treatment of women. They recognized that, unless equal pay and equal opportunity were the rule, some women would resent an increase in their contributions.

This proposal should, in my view, be given urgent attention. Discrimination in employment will continue as long as men are regarded as the principal breadwinners. Recognition of the value of the married woman's economic activity on domestic duties would help to bring about a change in attitudes.

But another change in our social insurance system should also be considered. At present every family is dependent on the father's earnings for the period when the mother is having a child. The present maternity allowance is usually paid for 18 weeks, starting 11 weeks before the confinement. This allowance is at the same rate as the flat sickness and unemployment benefits. Earnings related benefits are not attached. In addition, family allowance becomes due (but not for the first child). The total of these benefits is quite inadequate to prevent a serious fall in the family income during these periods. The period for which maternity allowance is paid is shorter than most people would agree as necessary to ensure the health of both child and mother.

It is widely felt that family allowances are too low. They have not been raised since 1968 and, at the least, they should be raised sufficiently to take account of the cost of living rise since then. The present allowance compares very unfavourably with those paid in the rest of the EEC. The purpose of the present allowance is to help cover the cost of bringing up a child. As such, it should be paid for the first child, raised to a more realistic level and reviewed annually. But a loss of income allowance is also needed by any family that has benefited from the wife's employment.

In 1970 the Government sought to meet this problem through the Family Income Supplement and no doubt, in so far as this has been a help to those in the lowest incomes, it has made a worthwhile contribution. But the more general problem remains and could only be met by an allowance available whenever the loss of income exceeds a minimum figure and where the family has benefited from this income for a minimum period.

This allowance should be paid for an extended period while the family is dependent on the father's earnings. The allowance could not be higher than the unemployment benefit, including earnings related benefit, but there seems no reason why it should not be at that level. It would, of course, replace the maternity allowance. The case for payment of this loss of income allowance is strengthened by the move to equal pay (see chapter 8).

There will probably be, many who will continue to object to any raising of family (ie child) allowances and, even more strongly, to a loss of income allowance on the ground that these benefits would encourage reproduction at a time when there is an urgent need to control (and, indeed, quickly reduce) world population growth. So far as I am aware, there is no statistical evidence to support the assumption that high birthrates are a consequence of improved standards of living and social benefits; on the contrary, it is not infrequently the underprivileged that have the highest reproduction rates, and there is evidence to support the view that differences in birthrates are to a considerable extent associated with unwanted pregnancies and a lack of family planning (see for example, *Family Policy*, Margaret Wynn).

Those who continue to urge this point of view overlook the serious consequences of deprivation, for children and society in general, whether absolute or relative, that must be associated with the loss of income associated with child-rearing (see chapter 2).

A more important objection is that married women

may be discouraged from re-entering employment. It is said that the single wage allowance in France tends to have this effect even though its value has not kept pace with the rise in the cost of living and the allowance is not now enough to compensate for the loss of earnings (see Report of Regional Trade Union Seminar, *Employment of Women*, Organisation for Economic Cooperation and Development [OECD] November 1968, pp 177–79).

This French allowance was introduced to give mothers a free choice between going out to work or devoting themselves solely to their family obligations; it has been paid so long as the family includes children and is dependent upon a single earner. An allowance intended to protect the family against loss of income as suggested above should only be paid for such period as is generally felt to be required to enable the mother to free herself for employment. Obviously, that period would depend upon whether or not the facilities for day-care referred to earlier in this chapter were being provided. The cost of providing these facilities would be balanced against the benefits of aiding the re-entry to employment; benefits in terms of confining payment of loss of income allowance for no more than is strictly necessary and in terms of expansion of the gross national product.

Taxation

The general income tax rule is that husband and wife are taxed as a single entity. The husband is assessed for tax on an income which includes the income of his wife. However, they can elect for separate assessments. This makes no difference to the total tax payable but it will ensure that tax is equitably apportioned. Until 1972, the only real concession was that the wife's earned income relief could be claimed against a working wife's own income but the wife's earnings were taken together with the husband's for assessment of surtax. As from the tax year 1972–73 this concession was extended to taxes on the higher rates and can be useful when the combined earnings exceed £5,000 (but it depends upon the proportion of total income contributed by each partner).

Investment income is still treated as a total and as the husband's income. In consequence, there are circumstances in which marriage increases the total liability to tax. Equally, there are circumstances when marriage can reduce the tax liability.

For estate duty purposes, husband and wife are treated as separate entities. This rule can cause real hardship but the recent decision to grant an additional exemption of £15,000 on any money left to the surviving spouse has reduced the number of such cases of hardship (See John Chown, *Financial Times* 15 12 73). The facilities now available for increasing income, by selling the house with a leaseback for life or purchasing an annuity, provide ways of mitigating this hardship.

In its evidence to the Select Committee, the Labour Party study group already quoted in this chapter pointed out that the present income tax rules failed to provide for equal treatment, because the husband is in law bound to declare his wife's income on his tax return and this requirement denies to the wife the privacy in financial affairs that her husband can still enjoy. The Study Group therefore recommended that the wife's income should be treated as her own, and personal relief for domestic and family obligations should be granted to those who actually fulfil them. The Study Group proposed that the married man's allowance should disappear and that even if the wife is not working the husband should get no more than the uniform allowance for which all would be eligible. This would increase the tax burden on couples unless they had children for whom proposed higher allowances would be available.

This proposal would seem to be more practicable if it were accompanied by the loss of earnings allowance proposed in the previous section.

It remains open to question whether the introduction

of separate treatment of incomes is the most appropriate at this time when an increasing number of women will be returning to employment after raising children. In other chapters of this book the desire to emphasize the joint responsibility for the family income has been noted; it seems that an increasing number of husbands and wives are viewing their roles and responsibilities in that light. It might be a mistake to change the income tax rules in a way that inhibited or at least discouraged them from taking that view. The right to separate assessment at the request of wife or husband should be assured but the alternative of combined assessment should be retained.

Relevant to this problem are the views put forward by Margaret Wynn in her study of the economic costs of rearing children. She has made a strong plea for family equity in preference to individual equity:

> "In its extreme form this old individualist principle held that every individual with the same income should be treated alike. Whether the individual, according to this principle, spends his income on maintaining a wife and raising a family, or stamp collecting, or breeding rabbits is irrelevant. Professor Titmuss notes that the more individual needs and dependencies are recognized, the more the principle of individual equity may fall into disrepute. . . . The broadening of the tax base to wage-earners of modest wages and the introduction of the Pay-As-You-Earn method of collection made it necessary to take account of family responsibilities, the second division of income. Individual equity ignores dependants or treats them like any other of a man's 'possessions'; family equity treats dependants as part-sharers in a man's income. The principle of individual equity ignores the social consequences, both short-term and long-term, of taxation or of income distribution on the family life cycle."
>
> Margaret Wynn, *Family Policy* p 197

Finance and legal responsibilities

The passing of the Women's Property Act in 1882, which gave married women the right to own and control property, was the first step in the slow progress towards full equality in the ownership of property. Under the Matrimonial Proceedings and Property Act 1970, a wife who has contributed to the acquisition or improvement of her husband's property may thereby acquire an interest in it. The Married Women's Property Act 1964 established that husband and wife are entitled to share equally savings from a housekeeping allowance made by the husband to the wife, or property acquired with such savings. But full equality in ownership of the matrimonial home is not yet assured; in its evidence to the Select Committee, the Labour Party Study Group referred to earlier put forward a number of proposals designed to achieve equal rights in this matter.

Discrimination against women in the use of financial facilities is general. Women generally have much more difficulty in raising loans, obtaining mortgages or hire-purchase facilities. In their evidence to the Select Committee, a number of organizations urged the need for legislation to remove this discrimination. The lack of equality in these matters must surely be a handicap.

Retirement and pensions

Discrimination in pensions has been repeatedly highlighted in the current debate and it is apparent that organizations representative of women are incensed that a lot of people seem to have adopted with little thought the present Government position that it:

> "does not believe that it is necessary to require occupational pension schemes to provide benefits for women and men on the same basis; thus the Social Security Act, which has passed through Parliament in the current session, will ensure that employed women as well as employed men are covered for earnings-related pensions from the start of the new arrangements in April 1975 but will not require identity of treatment, Many women will not wish to make the necessary payments."
>
> Equal Opportunities for Men and Women, para 2.8

Two of the main issues that need review are the

114

assumptions upon which pensions for women are generally based and the difference in treatment of widowers and widows.

On the first point, the key assumption is that, because women on average live longer than men, a smaller pension for them is actuarially necessary and therefore fair. The fact that women retire five years before men increases the difference in pensions by reducing the number of years' contributions. In occupational schemes, because the women's pension is on average paid for a longer period, the prospect that any pension reviews will keep pace with inflation is that much less likely (and in many schemes there is still no protection against inflation).

It is questionable whether the key assumption here is justified. Women undoubtedly on average live longer than men but some have a much shorter retirement than some men. The actuarial calculations are based on average probabilities. For example, a woman aged 20 has a 72 per cent probability of living to age 65, while the man at 20 has a 65 per cent probability of living to that age. But the average man or woman is rarely found, and since pensions for women are not, and could not be, related to individual life span, it seems quite unwarranted discrimination to vary the pension for women by any more than is made necessary by their present shorter working life.

On the second point, there can be no doubt that there are an increasing number of situations where the husband is just as dependent on the wife's earnings as the wife is on his, and the Government's assumption that "women might reasonably object to being obliged to contribute towards widowers' benefits on the same footing as men contribute towards widowhood cover", is at the least a quite un-warranted generalization. Provision should surely be made in both State and occupational schemes for widowers' benefits related to the wife's expectation of pension. For the present, it may be generally accepted that payment of contributions to cover this should not be compulsory, but it seems likely that time will see a change in attitude and acceptance of equal obligation to provide for the other partner. After all, nobody can predict the possibility of complete dependence of either partner on the other before retirement. The Social Security Act imposes a clear obligation on married men to provide a minimum widow's pension. There is no reason why married women should not similarly make provision for their husbands. The TUC has proposed that "in future there should be a next of kin benefit in the same way that the Principal Civil Service Pension Scheme now includes provision for death benefit to be payable to either spouse" (11 December 1973).

Until recently occupational schemes could only provide a widow's pension where it could be demonstrated that the husband was financially dependent on his wife, an invalid or otherwise incapable of self-support. A change in Inland Revenue rules now permits the provision of widowers' pensions on the same basis as for widows.

Finally, there is, of course, the difference in Normal Pension Date [NPD] which must surely be an obstacle for women seeking wider opportunities and, in particular, must be an additional handicap in promotion prospects. There is, understandably, little support for raising the women's NPD to 65, and much opposition, on grounds of costs, to lowering the men's NPD to 60. One solution, that would be welcomed by many men and women, is to enable both men and women to retire at any point between 60 and 65 (or even 70) with corresponding (but not crippling) adjustments of pension.

Awareness of some of the problems raised in this chapter has prompted proposals for a completely fresh approach to the determination of rights and benefits. Most people are dependent, to a degree at least, on the community while they are young and again when they retire from employment. Women are, in addition, dependent during pregnancy and child-rearing.

It has been suggested that the separate systems for

financing these periods of dependency could be combined through a central fund. Individuals would acquire rights to draw from the fund through taxation and insurance contributions. An advantage would be that individuals could have a choice of the form in which they exercised their drawing rights. It would enable those who wished to take a period for study (or extra holiday, perhaps) after some years of employment to do so without piling up debts. It would enable those who chose to save sufficient drawing rights to retire early or alternatively acquire an enhanced pension. The concept is an interesting one (for some discussion of these ideas see *New Patterns of Working Time*, OECD, 1973).

In the general debate about women's rights, attention has been drawn to the discrimination against women in occupational schemes. Some exclude them from membership, others exclude them until more years of service, or a higher minimum age than is required of men, have been met. In many schemes, part-time employees are excluded. The New Earnings Survey for 1970 showed that membership of occupational schemes was as follows:

Percentages of Employees in Schemes

	Men	*Women*		
		Full-time	*Part-time*	*Total*
Manual	46·2	17·9	3·4	11·9
Non-manual	74·5	47·4	6·3	38·6
Total	55·3	36·0	4·5	26·4

The TUC has proposed that "one of the criteria for recognition of an occupational pension scheme should be that it covers women employees equally with men and accords equal treatment to women within the scheme". However, because not all schemes would seek recognition, legislation should ensure equal treatment. (11 12 73) (p 3, para 13)

Sick pay

The New Earnings Survey for 1970 showed that discrimination against women in this matter was less than that concerning membership of pension schemes. Of more significance is the difference between the treatment accorded to part-time and full-time women workers on non-manual work. The figures were:

Percentages of employees provided with sick pay

	Men	Women		
		Full-time	*Part-time*	*Total*
Manual	63·4	46·7	51·8	48·8
Non-manual	92·6	89·2	57·2	82·3
Total	72·9	72·7	53·9	67·0

7 Government proposals

In September 1973 the Government published, in the form of a consultative document (*Equal Opportunities for Men and Women*, Department of Employment), proposals for legislation that would have the following objectives:
1 to widen the range of opportunities open to women
2 to help to remove unfair discrimination against women in such important areas as employment and training
3 to investigate the need for further measures including, if necessary, legislation to help women contribute to society on equal terms with men, thus opening fresh opportunities for both.

The proposals are of two kinds: measures to make certain acts of discrimination unlawful, and action by an Equal Opportunities Commission to extend the opportunities open to women.

Proposed measures

The proposed measures to make discrimination in employment on grounds of sex unlawful were seen by the Government as an essential complement to the Equal Pay Act 1970. The measures would make unlawful practices which "impede the progress of women and tend to restrict them to the less skilled and more poorly-paid jobs" and also provide "a new means of redress for individual women who feel they have suffered unfair discrimination in employment".

These proposals were published in response to the

growing demand for action by Government. The reports of the two parliamentary Select Committees in the House of Lords and the House of Commons, that heard evidence and reported their findings concerning Private Members Bills on the matter, had convinced the Government that "legislation was necessary and likely to be effective". Legislation alone will not secure reform, but, together with "educative and persuasive processes", offers the best prospects of bringing about change.

In the proposed Bill discrimination would be defined as "treating, on grounds of sex, one person less favourably than another". It would make it unlawful:

(1) To specify, in an advertisement, that only men or only women were required for a job.
(2) For employment agencies to discriminate in offering vacancies and submitting clients.
(3) For organizations offering courses of vocational training to people over school leaving age, to discriminate on the ground of sex in the provision of training facilities.
(4) To exclude a person from membership of, or from holding office in, a trade union or employers' association, on the ground of sex.

Non-discrimination would require equal treatment in terms of "access to potential benefits" and "protection against acts to their possible detriment". Accordingly equal treatment would be required in:

(1) Opportunities for recruitment, training, upgrading and promotion.
(2) Opportunities to earn more, "whether by working overtime or on shifts".
(3) Opportunities for whatever training or better-paid jobs are available within the firm (the Government suggests that this might be necessary in view of the present concentration of women in the less skilled and lower paid jobs).

120

(4) Protection against dismissal and in such matters as short-time, lay-offs and disciplinary measures.

Any marriage bar would become unlawful unless it applied also to men.

The proposed Bill would, as does the Equal Pay Act, provide for the exclusion from its effects of terms and conditions related to retirement, marriage and death, and equal treatment would not be required in so far as women may enjoy special terms and conditions related to pregnancy and child-rearing. Occupational pension schemes would not be required to provide benefits for men and women on the same basis (the Social Security Act 1973 does not require equal treatment, and indeed the State pension scheme will provide pensions on a different basis for men and women). However, the rules for approving schemes for tax purposes should be administered in such a way as to permit the same benefits to be provided. Since September 1973, (the Inland Revenue rules have been changed to allow this.)

The Bill would provide for specific and general exceptions. Specific exceptions would include employment in private households, clergy, armed forces, prison service and the police force. Present legislation requiring that particular tasks, mainly concerned with law enforcement, should be done by persons of one sex or the other, for example, search of persons by Customs and Excise Officers, would not be amended.

A general exception would be provided for cases where sex could be shown to be a genuine occupational qualification. The Government believes it is necessary to set out the criteria against which particular jobs should be judged, and proposes the following:

(a) Where the nature of the job requires it to be performed by a man (or woman) (eg foster-mother).
(b) Where the nature of the job necessarily requires a man or a woman in the interests of authenticity (eg acting).
(c) In forms of social work with people of both sexes, or in

mixed educational establishments, where it is necessary to maintain a team including persons of each sex (eg a team of probation officers).

(d) In single sex institutions where it could be shown that the employment of one sex only was legitimately related to the character of the institution (eg staff of convents).

(e) Where the nature of the employment makes it necessary to provide communal living accommodation (eg ships).

The intention was that, as each job about which a complaint had been raised was adjudicated on, a case law would be built up.

In addition to the above criteria for exceptions, the Government believed that there may be circumstances where a case might be made on the basis of the preference of those for whom the work in performed, eg

(a) Where it would be offensive to public taste or decency for a man (or a woman) to do the job.

(b) Where it could be shown that for the performance of personal services strong preferences among customers or clients made the employment of a man (or a woman) essential to the business.

The Government stated that it would not accept as justified any discrimination based on a difference in the cost of employing men or women, (or employing both rather than one sex only) or on a difference in rates of absenteeism or labour turnover. It also would not consider justified a discrimination adopted because the work would expose women to physical danger or adverse working conditions.

Small undertakings, initially defined as those employing not more than 25 people, would be excluded. The objects of charitable trusts would not be affected by the legislation. The proposed Bill would amend the Redundancy Payments Act and the Contracts of Employment Act so that a woman absent as a result of pregnancy or sickness would retain her continuity of employment if she began work again with the same employer within 26 weeks.

Enforcement

Complaints of unequal treatment would be referred to an Industrial Tribunal. (The Government undertook to bring about an increase in the number of women on the panels from which the Tribunals are drawn.) Cases would normally first be considered by the Department of Employment Conciliation Officers who already exercise similar functions in complaints of unfair dismissal and would deal with claims under the Equal Pay Act. Cases which could not be settled by conciliation would come before Industrial Tribunals. Where discrimination was established the Tribunals would make an order determining the rights of the parties, recommend a course of action and/or award compensation.

If an employer considered that he had been induced to discriminate by industrial action or the threat of industrial action, it would be open to him to join a trade union as a party to the proceedings as under section 119 of the Industrial Relations Act 1971, and the Tribunal could require the union to contribute an appropriate share of any compensation awarded. Where a Tribunal considered that a case had been brought frivolously or vexatiously, it could impose an appropriate order for costs. Important cases concerning, for example, advertisements or employment agencies could be transferred to the National Industrial Relations Court.

As in the Equal Pay Act, provision would be made for the Secretary of State for Employment to make a reference on a woman's behalf where it was not reasonable to expect her to refer the matter herself to a Tribunal.

Restriction on hours etc and protective legislation

The Government also intended to repeal those restrictions in the Factories Act 1961 and associated legislation relating to hours of employment, including overtime,

Sunday and night work and those relating to moving machinery. Restriction on hours of work for women working above ground laid down in the Mines and Quarries Act 1954 would also be repealed.

The Government believed these restrictions were no longer appropriate and would be used by employers as justification for treating a wide field of employment as an exception from the Bill's requirements.

The restrictions related to maternity protection would continue. The Government believed that a case for repeal of some of the restrictions imposed on health and other grounds might be made. These include:

(a) the prohibition under the Mines and Quarries Act of working underground by women, and

(b) the power conferred by the Midwives Act 1951 on the Central Midwives Board to issue certificates of enrolment as midwives only to women.

The Government believed public opinion might nevertheless favour the retention of these restrictions.

The Equal Opportunities Commission

The Commission [EOC] would have powers "to conduct wide ranging inquiries into the relative positions and opportunities of men and women, to publish its findings in the form of reports to the Government and to educate and persuade public opinion". It would work by securing voluntary cooperation, persuasion and publicity and it would be open to the Commission to propose further measures, including legislation, to remedy particular situations of inequality. It would have no power to enforce its recommendations.

The Government assumed that the Commission would spend a substantial part of its time on employment matters, but it would be open to it to propose to the Government that it should investigate "other areas of concern", including education. The Government proposed that the Commission should at an early stage carry out "an examination

124

into the relative positions and opportunities of men and women within the professions".

In employment, complaints could be followed up by local inquiries or more general investigations. Investigations into individual organizations would not be ruled out. In investigations approved by the Government, the Commission "would have powers of inquiry covering the production of documents, summoning of witnesses, and the conduct of statistical inquiries." The Commission "could act as a catalyst by encouraging local campaigns and sponsoring local conferences of careers officers, careers teachers and others with the aim of changing the traditional attitudes often found among employers, young persons and parents towards employment and training of women and girls. Such action could help to break the present vicious circle in which employers do not recruit girls because so few suitable candidates come forward, and suitable girls do not apply because so few employers, they believe, are willing to take them on. It was expected that the Commission would pay careful attention to examples of good practice in employment and to disseminating them among employers, as well as indicating the areas where improvement was most needed."

Education

The Government, having noted the evidence presented to the Parliamentary Select Committees, thought that there was need to "take action to ensure that discrimination on grounds of sex does not occur in the field of education". It did not intend to include such action in the proposed Bill (but, as a field of employment for teachers and others, education would not be exempted from operation of the Bill). The Government believed that Ministers already had sufficient powers to deal with discrimination in educational establishments.

Instead the Government proposed:

(1) "To ask Her Majesty's Inspectors to undertake a study

125

of the extent to which curricular differences and customs contribute to unequal opportunities for boys and girls. This study would cover single sex and mixed schools and would indicate whether any changes were necessary."

(2) To "discuss with careers officers and careers teachers the role they can play" in "encouraging young women to consider careers traditionally taken up by men and vice versa".

(3) To begin immediate discussions with universities "to establish how they could best respond to the need to avoid any discrimination on grounds of sex in their admissions policy". (It was noted that the Select Committee had not taken broadly based evidence from the authorities responsible for universities.)

(4) Education would be included "with other broad areas in the Commission's duty to investigate and report on matters of general concern in relation to discrimination on grounds of sex".

Comment on the Proposals

The Government's proposals were generally welcomed but there has been strong criticism on the following aspects:

(1) All matters relating to financial and legal responsibilities had been omitted. The Government had failed to recognize the need for changes in every sphere where discrimination is helping to maintain an inferior status for women. Equal opportunity in employment will not be easy to achieve but it will be unobtainable if discrimination based on an outmoded view of women's role in family and society is retained. Much will, therefore, depend upon how realistically the Government determines priorities for investigation by the EOC into other areas of concern.

(2) Matters relating to retirement, marriage and death will be excluded. The major objection here is to the continued discrimination in pensions and retirement. A discussion of this matter is included in chapter 6. Now that occupa-

tional schemes are permitted to provide widowers' pensions on the same basis as widows' pensions, there will be criticism of those which fail to make use of this change in the rules. There is concern also at the continued disparity in membership of occupational schemes, and it has been urged by the TUC and others that legislation to ensure equal right to membership is needed.

So far as determination of pensions on an actuarial basis is concerned, the main criticism should be directed at Government policy and at the provisions of the Social Security Act in particular. Most occupational schemes do not base pensions for men and women on different formulae. Of course, the difference in NPD remains contentious and affects pensions. That is discussed in chapter 6.

(3) The provision of criteria for exceptions has met with heavy criticism. It has been said that "the full list of proposed exceptions taken together would so undermine the principle of equality as to make it meaningless and needs to be radically altered" (GMWU). The TUC has stated that "the only category whose exclusion from the scope of the legislation is acceptable to the General Council is that of the clergy and religious orders" (TUC 11 12 73). The IPM has suggested that the list of criteria be substituted by a clause which "would require the employer *in each case* to show special and exceptional reasons within the contents of the job why exemption under the proposed law should be allowed".

The inclusion in the criteria of phrases like "where it would be offensive to public taste or decency" and "where it could be shown that for the performance of personal services strong preferences among customers or clients made the employment of a man (or woman) essential to the business" shows a lack of understanding of our problem. To rely on current attitudes to determine where discrimination should be permitted is absurd. The objective is to change those attitudes not to enshrine them in case law.

(4) The proposal for continuity of employment following pregnancy (or sickness) provided work is resumed within 26 weeks is generally welcomed. But the other issues raised in chapter 5 remain to be dealt with. In particular, the right to reinstatement and protection against dismissal because of pregnancy have been urged and these are matters demanding thorough investigation.

(5) A good deal of controversy has been stirred up by the Government's proposal to repeal most of the statutory restrictions on the employment of women. In the Government booklet a good case for this proposal has been made. It is unfortunate that some have regarded it as a *quid pro quo* for the other measures proposed. The TUC's position is that:

> "where there is considered to be a case for amending or relaxing any restrictions, any change in working conditions in individual establishments must not be made without consultation with, and the agreement of, the trade unions and the women workers concerned. This would particularly apply to the lifting of the prohibition on night work by women which must not be removed until equal pay is fully implemented and unions and workers are prepared to accept such a radical change (conditions which are not generally applicable at the present time)".

para 25, 11 12 73

The Vice-President of the National Union of Hosiery and Knitwear Workers made a statement recently which showed how better job opportunity for women can be dependent upon repeal of the legislation. He feared that repeal would remove a necessary protection for women, but went on to say that:

> "women do not do any of the skilled jobs in the hosiery or knitwear industries, except for a tiny minority who have been doing the jobs since the war and have not yet retired. The fundamental reason for this is that employers need to obtain a special licence in order to employ women on a three-shift basis. There are as many knitting machines

around as there are men to operate them, if you see what I mean".

Guardian 9/11/73

(6) Trade union comments on the proposals for enforcement arise to some extent from their concern not to depend upon the tribunals and the National Industrial Relation Court while the Industrial Relations Act remains on the statute book. The TUC has suggested that "it would be preferable for claims (concerning equal pay and equal opportunity) to be heard by a panel of industrial arbitrators" who would have "adequate knowledge of industry and its processes" (11 12 73).

Writing in *Personnel Management* (November 1973), Baroness Seear [Nancy Seear] supported the Government's proposal to separate the tasks of education and enforcement – "the most effective teachers do not wield a big stick" – and suggested that a special agency, independent of Government departments, should be set up to provide assistance to those who need it. "It is very difficult to prove discrimination, especially in the key area of promotion, and it is easy to become unpopular with both employer and colleagues in the attempt. Individual women will need a great deal of help and encouragement in presenting cases . . . Moreover, where a case is successfully fought, damages should be on a scale to make the effort worthwhile for the claimant, and to be a deterrent to the discriminator." (The Government had given no indication of penalties to be levied.)

Comments by the Race Relations Board

The Race Relations Board has submitted its views on the Government's proposals for enforcement of the legislation. The comments are based on the Board's experience in operating the Race Relations Act 1968 and as such will be given serious consideration.

The Board's views are based on the proposition that the legislation should have three objectives:

(1) to provide effective redress for the individual victim of discrimination

(2) to prevent future discrimination by a person held to have discriminated, and

(3) to eliminate patterns of discrimination which may not become the subject of individual complaints.

In the Board's view the Government's proposal will not provide the means to achieve these objectives. The proposals were considered under three headings: the complaints process; powers for tackling patterns of discrimination; recommendations for legislation.

Complaints process

The main criticism here is the absence of any provision for an independent investigation to establish the facts of a complaint (the point made by Nancy Seear quoted above). The complainant would have to bear much of the burden of proving discrimination and rebutting defences.

The complainant would have to show:

"that some action to his or her detriment . . . had occurred and that there were reasonable grounds for believing *that the action had been taken by reason of his or her sex*. This being shown, it would then be for the employer to prove the contrary." (Quoted from Government proposals)

This requirement is in direct contrast to the Race Relations Act 1968 and the Industrial Relations Act 1971 which require only an allegation of an unlawful act, and to the Redundancy Payments Act 1965, which specifically requires Tribunals to make a presumption in favour of the claimant, unless the respondent proves the dismissal not to have been by reason of redundancy. The TUC has also made this point (11 12 73).

One might add that in the Equal Pay Act the onus is on the employer to show that the advantage (enjoyed by another with whom equal treatment has been claimed) is genuinely due to a material difference (other than the difference of sex).

The process of fact-finding and comparison is not

likely to be efficiently carried out in a hearing. An investigation by an independent agency is needed. No arrangements for legal aid are proposed, and without legal aid a complainant will often be at a serious disadvantage. The legislation should provide protection against victimization. The proposals contain no means of placing on the respondent a requirement to take steps to prevent future discrimination (however the matter is settled).

Patterns of discrimination

Discrimination cannot be effectively tackled by a complaints process alone. Discrimination in employment must

be seen not just in terms of individual acts of discrimination, but in terms of employment situations in which equality of opportunity is consciously or unconscisiouly denied.

The proposals suggest that such patterns can best be changed through education and persuasion based on general enquiries and reports. While the Board recognizes the long-term value of education and persuasion in changing attitudes on which inequality of opportunity is based, it is thought essential that powers be available directly to bring about change in patterns of discrimination. The Race Relations Act provides limited powers for the Board to initiate investigations where discrimination is suspected but no formal complaint has been made. The consultative document suggests no such powers for any agency dealing with sex discrimination, and limits the powers of the proposed Equal Opportunities Commission to advising complainants of their rights, and to 'local enquiries' which could lead to no direct enforcement efforts. Further, the Commission is to be dependent on the government for permission to undertake general enquiries."

Recommendations

The Board therefore recommends that discrimination on the ground of sex should be dealt with by an independent agency which should have power to investigate and settle individual complaints, and power to tackle patterns of discrimination. It should have powers, not presently available to the Race Relations Board, to secure disclosure of documents and attendance of witnesses, to compel respondents to take steps to prevent discrimination, to make follow-up checks and power to compel respondents to keep the records required to show whether discrimination has stopped.

The Board also recommends that the agency should have power to investigate an organization where there are allegations that "a more general situation of long-term unequal opportunity" (para 4.5 of the Government document) exists.

It should have power to make a conciliation agreement which should be legally enforceable. The power to undertake such investigations should not depend on Government permission.

Claims under the Equal Pay Act should be transferred from the Industrial Tribunals to the agency.

The Board does not accept the argument advanced in favour of separating enforcement from education and persuasion. It sees no reason therefore why the proposed Equal Opportunities Commission should not be the agency which the Board recommends. The Board sees no reason why the Commission should be required to seek Government approval for its enquiries. If that view is not acceptable, then the criteria on which Government approval is, or is not, given should be clearly stated and published.

If an independent agency is not set up, legal aid should be available for complainants or, alternatively, a body established to advise and represent complainants (similar to that set up under immigration appeals procedures). Means should be devised to allow a requirement to be placed on respondents to prevent future discrimination.

Timing of legislation

In September 1973 the Government said that it intended to introduce its proposed Bill in the current session. It would therefore have been on the Statute Book before the

Equal Pay Act comes into force at the end of 1975. This intention was welcomed by many who have feared the effects of the Equal Pay Act on women's opportunities. We must remember that, as the CBI pointed out in its evidence to the Select Committee, " . . . one great advantage to the employer of employing women will be considerably diminished in many cases with the implementation of the Equal Pay Act". It is for this reason that the IPM has urged that the proposed legislation be implemented before the end of 1975. The CBI has also urged that the legislation should be closely linked with the Equal Pay Act and become operative at the end of 1975.

8 The move towards equal pay

1 A Re-assessment of the Problems

In the course of the debate leading to passing of the Equal Pay Act 1970, a number of problems that would arise in implementation were identified. Further thought and experience since then has modified the concern on some of these. On some, it is now thought the problem has been exaggerated; on others, that the gravity of the problem has still not been sufficiently recognized. And on others again, because the Act is not yet in force, we know little more than in 1970. The following problems were identified during the debate.

Same work or *work of equal value*

The debate started from the assumption that a choice had to be made between equal pay for the same work or equal pay for work of equal value. In the event, the Labour Government decided to cater for both possibilities, ie equal pay for 'like work' and equal pay for 'equally rated work' where job evaluation is used to determine pay and conditions of employment (see Appendix 30 for a brief summary of the Act).

The debate has therefore turned to other problems. How will like work be interpreted? In the Act, the following phrases are relevant – "of the same or broadly similar nature"; "the differences between the things she does and the things they (ie men) do are not of practical importance in relation to terms and conditions of employment"; "regard shall be had to the frequency or otherwise with which any such differences occur in practice as well as to the nature and extent of the differences" Clause 1 (4).

The interpretation of these phrases by Industrial Tribunals will be important in determining the rate of progress to equal pay. In the meantime, speculation continues.

The Act does not require a company to use job evaluation but, if terms and conditions for both men and women are determined by job evaluation, the scheme must not set "different values for men and women on the same demand under any heading". There will no doubt be differences of view about what these words mean.

There may also be differences of view about the area of work to be covered by any evaluation system. Skilled work is often separated from unskilled and semi-skilled work, and production jobs from ancillary jobs. Sometimes there are separate systems for each department, for example, engineering (maintenance etc), assembly, foundry etc. In the staff area, technical work is often separated from clerical, factory supervision from office supervision and so on. Again, shift workers are sometimes separated from day workers and full-time workers. The acceptability of such divisions has up to now depended a good deal upon whether they fitted in with organization in different unions. Their effects on equal pay implementation will now be an additional factor, and this could induce some difficult and potentially bitter manoeuvering for position.

The original problem remains unresolved. What is the most practicable, constructive and acceptable basis for implementation? One thing is clear. In so far as the like work basis is used, there will be a segregation of women into those (relatively few) who do work that is accepted to be like that performed by men, and the majority who do work that is traditionally accepted as women's work. There can be no doubt that in many companies much of the women's work would rate higher in any fair evaluation than the like work. Indeed, in the unequal pay situation it is not uncommon to find that women on like work are paid less than some of those on women's work. For this reason, some companies have resisted pressure for implementation on the like work basis, preferring to accept the higher cost of a wider and more fair implementation on a job evaluation basis.

It is relevant here to draw attention to advice given by the Engineering Employer's Federation [EEF] to its member firms. Following a comprehensive review of every aspect of employment in the company, they should decide whether "job evaluation would facilitate implementation and so reduce the number of claims that could be made on grounds of job comparability . . . Despite the disadvantages, the use of a single, easily understood job evaluation scheme will greatly assist in the introduction of equal pay . . . " There can be no doubt that the use of job evaluation can help to provide the basis for constructive relations in a company.

The Industrial Society recently published the results of a survey on the implementation of the Equal Pay Act. The survey covered 96 of the Society's member firms employing a total of 470,000 people (including 131,000 women). Nearly half the companies already have job evaluation schemes in operation (and most of these schemes are common to both male and female jobs). Nearly one-third of those which do not have a job evaluation scheme are planning to introduce one. For many companies, a decision about use of job evaluation needs to be based on a thorough review of the wage structure and related matters (as the EEF suggested). Since there are commonly fairly high costs involved in implementing the changes in differentials (between male categories as much as between men and women generally) a decision based on the equal pay problem alone would be unwise.

Of course, now that the need to take a fresh look at the

136

division of work between men and women is being strengthened by the prospect of an Equal Opportunities Act, job evaluation has an added attraction because it can provide the basis for such a fresh look.

It seems that some fears have been aroused in trade unions that job evaluation may be used to minimize the effect of the Act by changing the work content of some jobs and down-grading them (see, for example, *The Sunday Times* report, 4 2 73). That could happen, but most companies today would be unlikely to contemplate use of job evaluation unless they could be confident of cooperation from representatives in the exercise. The trade union interest in this matter was well expressed by a representative of the National Joint Committee of Working Women's Organizations in response to a question about progress in implementation of the Equal Pay Act from a member of the House of Commons Sub-Committee on the Employment of Women:

> "If you are thinking about simply the abolition of women's rates, obviously we are making progress on that, and I think very good progress . . . But as far as equal pay for work of equal value is concerned, which where we really aim to make progress . . . because of the very few who are doing the same work as men, . . . I am reserving judgement . . . You can get equal pay for people doing identical jobs perhaps in the same scale that has been set out, but to get women's jobs classified as being of as high a grade, or higher in some cases, is where the problem begins."

> SBN 218273 p 82

Finally, it is relevant to point out that in June 1971 the Government ratified the International Labour Office [ILO] Convention No 100 which provides that member countries shall "ensure the application to all workers of the principle of equal remuneration for men and women workers for work of equal value". The Government evidently did not attach any significance to the words 'work of equal value'.

Speaking on that occasion, Robert Carr said:

> "We have been able to do this because the Equal Pay Act, which was passed last year with the support of both Government and Opposition, requires the full introduction of equal pay in all sectors of employment by the end of 1975, and a number of industries and firms are already making adjustments towards this goal in their wage settlements."

Press release 15 6 71

Definition of equal value

There has been much debate about what conditions have to be met for work to be of equal value. Differences in output between one worker and another present no great problem because wage systems generally make some provision for an element of payment-by-results wherever output or performance can be measured or assessed. At least, if there is a problem, it is not one that arises from the Equal Pay Act as such. The major debate has been over the contention by many employers that because the absenteeism of women is, on average, higher than that of men, because women are not so readily available for overtime and because of the legal restrictions on their hours and shift arrangements, their work is held not to be, on average, of equal value to that of men.

The debate continues but the unfairness of the argument is much more widely admitted today. Differences in the absence record of men do not, generally at least, affect their rate of pay and the level of absence of some men is much higher than that of some women. Mere preparedness to work overtime or to transfer from day work to shift work does not qualify a man to receive a higher level of pay. Differences in the cost of employing one person or other are important but those differences exist between one man and another as much as between a man and a woman. The sex differential has been an extremely clumsy and inequitable device and its disappearance will enable a more rational consideration of the real problem. In so far as more equal opportunity widens the area of common employment for men and women, it can help employers to select and retain those men or women best able to meet the requirements of the job. Under the Industrial Relations Act, dismissal on grounds of a persistently high or unreasonable level of absence may be judged fair, provided proper warnings have been given (see also proposal for a 'less demanding contract' in chapter 6).

Equal pay in staff areas

Because there is a large discretionary element in most non-manual salary structures, the move towards equal pay is much more difficult to plan and monitor than in manual work employment. Indeed it is often difficult to define the extent to which a sex differential exists at present – not that the existence of a differential in general is in doubt. Indeed, because flexibility allows the market pressures to operate more effectively in staff areas, it is probable that the differential is wider for most non-manual work than for manual work and in consequence, as the Act is implemented we may well see the rates for women on manual work rising at a faster rate than the salaries of women on non-manual work (particularly where manual work is covered by a job evaluation system).

The Act will require an employer to demonstrate, in the event that there is a claim that equal treatment is not being given, that any difference between a man or a woman on like work or equally rated work is not due to the difference of sex. Such a difference in salary might arise from an assessed difference in performance and as such is often at best very difficult to account for in objective terms meaningful to those not directly concerned, and at worst quite inexplicable except to the individual making the assessment. The need for more systematic methods of assessment is already growing with the steadily growing involvement of staff unions in salary determination; the move to equal pay is increasing the pressure for this change.

As with so many other features of human society,

flexibility is indivisible. If system replaces discretion in one element of salary determination, for example, a performance or merit addition, then inevitably system must be introduced into the others, ie the determination of grades, any regional differences, market pressure supplements, otherwise each of these becomes an escape route for reintroducing the lost 'discretion'.

Definition of same employment

The Act requires that women be given "equal treatment with men in the same employment", ie "men employed by her employer or any associated employer at the same establishment or at establishments in Great Britain which include that one and at which common terms and conditions of employment are observed either generally or for employees of the relevant classes". (Clause 1(2))

This clause created a good deal of alarm amongst employers generally. Did this mean that a woman in, say, Scotland, could claim equal treatment with men in, say, London if they were all employed by the same company or group of associated companies? Authoritative answers cannot be given. The Tribunals will have to decide if a claim on this basis is made. Responsible Ministers of the Labour Government, which introduced the Bill, declared that they had no intention of providing legislative support for parity claims. There may be attempts to use the Act in support of such claims but it seems most unlikely that they would be successful. Provided men in different plants of a group are paid differently, there is no reason why women also should not be paid differently. Of course, if men already have parity, women may also be able to obtain parity.

There has been a good deal of puzzlement also concerning the interpretation that may be given to the words "and at which common terms and conditions of employment are observed". Supposing some are common and others not? Would a difference in, say, the shift system be relevant? The only point that does seem to be clear is that if the only difference is in the rate of pay then that difference may have to disappear too (except where a comparison within the plant takes precedence over comparison between plants).

Inflation of wage claims

Some fears were expressed in 1970 that, because the additional increases for women that would be required to close the gap were in many cases substantial, there would be a demand from men for a higher level of general increases. It was suggested, for example, that it was unlikely that men would accept a level of general settlement which meant that women obtained twice the increase given to men. In practice, we shall now it seems never know whether this fear was realistic or not, because the general increases that were accompanied by equal pay moves have been considerably larger than was envisaged when the Act was passed; it seems unlikely that the pace of inflation could be reduced in the next two years to a level where this problem again becomes real. It could be argued that the equal pay moves have contributed to the inflation and confirmed the fears.

Consequential claims

Fears have also been expressed that claims would be pressed for increases in overtime pay, shift allowances and other elements in the pay packet that would benefit men rather than women. As yet, there does not seem any substantial evidence that would show that these fears had been justified. Claims for such increases are not new and we can expect that they will be pressed as hard in the future as in the past, but it seems likely that the fears may have been exaggerated. It could also be argued that, since the gap between men's pay and women's pay has not been closed, and that in many fields of employment the gap, in terms of the Act, has not even been defined (see the second part of this chapter), it is much too soon to assess the effect of the

Act on men's demands.

Effect on costs

The gap between men's pay and women's pay for work that may be deemed to be 'like', or for work rated as equal under job evaluation, has varied considerably. In 1970, cases where the gap was 40 per cent of the man's pay were not difficult to find, but just as common were cases where the gap was 25 per cent or less. Not surprisingly, therefore, the effect of the Act on costs has been one of the greatest worries not only of employers but also of some women employees, who have feared that they would be squeezed out of employment in consequence (a fear which is also discussed in chapter 6).

In the event, the rate of inflation has risen to such an extent since 1970 that assessment of the impact of equal pay moves has seemed unimportant by comparison with other factors. It is in any case too soon to make an assessment of any value, because the pace of movement to equal pay up to now has varied considerably between industries and indeed within some industries, particularly the engineering and allied industries.

A recent survey by the Industrial Society provided cost estimates from 35 companies. Ten estimated the cost of equal pay at less than 1 per cent of the payroll; 15 estimated it would be between 1 per cent and 5 per cent and seven that it would cost between 6 per cent and 10 per cent. Only one company estimated the cost at more than 20 per cent; 34 companies could not provide an estimate and another 27 did not answer the question. More than 60 per cent of the companies therefore either had no estimate as yet or do not consider it important to make an estimate. Without doubt there are still many companies who have no idea what is required of them.

One encouraging development over this period has been the increasing attention being paid to measures that can help industry to bear the cost of equal pay. Cost reduction and manpower utilization investigations have no doubt been given something of a boost by the realization that cheap woman power would no longer be available. Some employers have also been aware of the fact that the requirements of the Equal Pay Act were going to have a larger effect on wage costs here than legislation in other EEC countries seems to have had.

Equal pay without equal opportunity

Reference has already been made to the fear that some women have had of unemployment as an outcome of equal pay. Others have feared that there would be increased efforts to create special women's jobs as a means of avoiding the effect of the requirements of the Act. This fear led to a demand that equal pay legislation should be accompanied by equal opportunity legislation. The matter was raised in the Committee stage on the Equal Pay Bill and the point was put by Robert Carr:

> There is a real danger that if we press hard on the door of equal pay, without at the same time pressing hard to push open the door of equal opportunity, we shall create a situation where we intensify this hiving-off tendency of women's employment, and, although we might get equal pay for very large numbers of women, it would be low pay. If the Bill does nothing about equality of opportunity, it might fail to help a large majority of women workers and make advancement in pay and job opportunity more difficult rather than less difficult."

Standing Committee on the Equal Pay (No 2) Bill 3 3 70

It has been just as strongly argued that unequal opportunity will remain so long as there is unequal pay. In its evidence to the Royal Commission on Trade Unions and Employers' Associations the Amalgamated Engineering Union (now the Amalgamated Union of Engineering Workers) said:

> "So long as women are paid less wages than men for no other reason than that they are women, men will always be inclined to insist on a demarcation between men's and women's work.

They are compelled to do this in order to protect their own wage standards."

Both arguments lend support to the growing body of opinion in favour of the proposed legislation on equal opportunity coming into effect at the end of 1975.

How far the move to equal pay has, or will have, any effect on the opportunities for women we still do not know. The evidence quoted in the second part of this chapter suggests that in many companies the change in wage rates and in overall labour costs resulting from the Equal Pay Act, though substantial, is not large relative to the overall inflation, and there are still a good many companies that have made no moves or have not decided what they intend to do.

Effect on family incomes

The move to equal pay will have the effect of reducing the share of earned income going to the families that are dependent on the husband's earnings, as all families are for a period depending on the number of children being reared. It is possible that the overall cost of equal pay can be met out of an increase in gross national product, in which case the loss to these families will only be a relative one. But it is possible, indeed quite probable, that gross national product will not rise sufficiently to meet the cost of equal pay, particularly now that we have additional heavy external costs to meet. In that event, the standard of living of these families will fall absolutely.

In chapter 6 a case is made for a loss of income allowance to be paid for a limited period to mothers who leave employment for a period to bring up children. Such an allowance, coupled with a substantial increase in the family (ie child) allowance is needed to ensure that families do not suffer a fall in their standard of living.

2 An assessment of prospects

How much movement in Pay has there been so far ?

In August 1972 the Office of Manpower Economics reported that in about one-fifth of the national agreements and wages council orders covering manual workers (and about one-third of the total number of women covered by such agreements and orders) discrimination in rates of pay had been removed or a commitment had been undertaken for its phased removal by the end of 1975 or earlier.

But about one-in-nine of female manual workers was affected by agreements or orders in which no move towards equal pay had occurred and in which the minimum rates for women were still less than 80 per cent of men's.

At company level, about one-fifth of those surveyed by staff of the Office had introduced equal pay for either manual or non-manual employees but only one-in-ten had done so for both. A further quarter had definite plans for implementing the Act. In contrast, more than two-fifths of the companies had neither taken action to introduce equal pay nor had planned to do so. Progress had been distinctly greater for white-collar than for manual workers.

In a separate survey of some 200 small companies (ie with less than 100 employees) not subject to collective bargaining or wages council orders, only four were found to have made plans to introduce equal pay, although 35 claimed that equal pay already operated. In July 1973, Incomes Data Services reported on its third study of women's pay. An examination of national agreements showed that the following progress had been made, on average:

	Women's rate as percentage of male rate	*Cash differential*
Mid-1972	85·1%	£2·24
Mid-1973	87·5%	£2·02

The progress in 1972–3 was slightly less than in the previous year. If the percentage differential were not closed at a faster rate than 2·5 per cent per year, another five years would have to pass before the differential were removed. A much larger movement, on average will be needed in 1974 and 1975 to meet the requirements of the Act concerning collective agreements.

A disturbing fact, also reported by IDS, was that 49 out of 84 industry agreements in the private sector provided a women's rate below 90 per cent of the male rate and in five of these the women's rate was below 80 per cent of the men's. (IDS Study No 56, July 1973)

In another report, the minimum rates laid down for 101 groups covered by national agreements were analysed. This showed that women's rates had, on average, increased from 86·2 per cent of the minimum male rate at February 1973 to 89·4 per cent at the end of November 1973. Excluding 15 groups which have reached 100 per cent, the average had risen from 84·0 per cent to 88·5 per cent as a result of Stage II settlements, and the differentials were as follows:

$$
\begin{array}{rcl}
4-\ 5\% & - & 3 \text{ agreements} \\
6-10\% & - & 35 \text{ agreements} \\
11-15\% & - & 26 \text{ agreements} \\
16-20\% & - & 18 \text{ agreements} \\
21-25\% & - & 4 \text{ agreements}
\end{array}
$$

An earlier study had shown that, with the increases permitted under Stage II (see below), the number remaining below 90 per cent should have been 37. There were in fact 48 and it seems that some had either taken no advantage of the Stage II provision or had not used it to the full. (*Industrial Relations Review and Report*, No 69, December 1973)

In spite of the evidence that progress was slow and uneven, the Secretary of State decided not to use the powers provided in the Equal Pay Act to require that by the end of 1973 a woman's rate of pay should be not less than 90 per cent of the rate paid to a man, with whom equality will be required at the end of 1975. Instead, provision was made under Stage II of the Counter-Inflation Programme for additional increases to be paid to women in order to close the differential by one-third. There has been much criticism of this decision and the argument will continue about whether more progress would have been achieved had the powers been used. One fact is clear. Whichever course had been taken, there are still many companies where the amount of movement required would have been undefined because there had been no decision as to the position which must be reached at the end of 1975.

Industrial Relations Review and Report recently obtained answers to a questionnaire from 66 subscribers. Nine of them have already introduced equal pay for either all groups of workers or at least for those groups in which women are mainly employed. Of the remaining 57, 24 companies have at least certain groups on equal pay, most in staff areas. But in 33 companies, no groups are yet receiving equal pay. Forty-five of these 66 companies have now agreed plans for phasing in equal pay by the end of 1975. Five have no plans to date. Job evaluation is being used or being considered by only a very small number. Twenty of the companies yet to implement full equality plan to do so earlier than the end of 1975.

During Stage II, 14 of these 16 companies failed to take any advantage at all of the provision for an additional increase for women. A further 12 did not give the maximum possible. In 29 of these companies some women are paid at the 90 per cent level but the majority are paid at the 80 per cent to 90 per cent level and there are still some at 75 per cent or lower. (*Industrial Relations Review and Report* No 70, December 1973)

The Industrial Society carried out a similar survey in June 1973. It was on the same lines as the 1971 survey and showed that, in the companies taking part in both, the differential had narrowed significantly. In 1971 about one-third had a differential greater than 20 per cent; in 1973 only one company had such a large differential. In 1971, none of the companies had a differential of 5 per cent or less; by 1973 one-tenth of these companies had reduced their differential to this level.

In the 1973 survey, 18 of the 96 companies were unable to say what the differential was; 26 reported that they were already providing equal pay (ten of these were in insurance or banking). In the remaining 52 companies the differential was:

1– 5%	—	7
6–10%	—	22
11–15%	—	14
16–20%	—	8
21–25%	—	–
26–30%	—	1
	TOTAL	52

(*Industrial Society, Survey and Report* No 184, November 1973)

It thus seems that, since 1971, significant moves towards equal pay have been made by many companies and that the basis upon which equal pay will be introduced by the end of 1975 has also been decided in many companies. But there is a significant minority that have given the matter little if any attention at all.

So far as national agreements are concerned, more than 10 per cent now meet the requirements of the Act but more than half (at December 1973) had a differential of more than 10 per cent. Stage III increases have still to be implemented in many of the industries covered by these agreements and settlements within the Pay Code should bring a further significant closing of the gap. There may again be some industries which fail to make full use of the latitude provided.

What are the prospects?

It seems likely that a good many companies are assuming that, provided they implement any change required of them by a new national agreement, no other demands would be made on them. For some, that is almost certainly a mistaken view of what the Act requires. National agreements generally lay down minimum rates but actual pay levels, particularly for men, are often in advance of the agreed minimum. In engineering, for example, pay structures for all categories of men on manual work are generally well in advance of national minima and, because men employees are more in demand than women, the difference between the minimum and the actual rate is generally greater for men than women.

In engineering, there is the additional and important fact that in the national agreement there is no minimum for the considerable number of semi-skilled men with whom equality of treatment can be claimed by many of the women employed. The Act requires that the national women's rate should disappear at the end of 1975 and the male unskilled rate will then be the agreed minimum for both men and women. There need be no doubt that the national agreement will be changed to meet this requirement and that, in consequence, women in many firms in the industry will get special increases to meet the new commonly applied minimum. But many of the women are employed on semi-skilled work, and equal treatment with men for them can only be assured by the application of those clauses of the Act relating to 'an employer's pay structure' and to a comparison of the work performed by men and women.

Similar problems will arise in other industries and it is therefore probable that during 1975 the Industrial Arbitration Board will be asked (under Clause 10 of the Act) to declare what amendments may be needed in agreements on pay structures to provide equal treatment by the end of 1975.

Finally, the Act requires equal treatment in matters

other than pay. Pensions and some other matters are excluded (see Appendix 30) but there are a number of conditions of employment where differences of treatment have not been uncommon. For example, payment during sickness (see chapter 6), rest and fatigue allowances in payment-by-result schemes, cleaning-up or washing time at the end of the day. Wherever equal pay is required by the Act, any such differences in treatment must disappear and claims can, and will no doubt, be made by men where women retain an advantage on a matter that is covered by the Act.

Incidentally, contrary to the interpretation adopted by some people, the Act does not provide justification for unequal pay where current legislation prevents an employer from requiring women to work the same hours as men. The effect of Clause 6(1) is to exclude claims from men for equal treatment with women whose employment conditions are restricted by law.

What are the main obstacles?

The main obstacles to a wider and more rapid implementation of equal pay seem to be:

(1) Pre-occupation of both employers and unions with other, more pressing problems. An Act of Parliament does not automatically change people's social and economic priorities.

(2) Indifference, ignorance and lack of understanding about what the Act requires and the scope it offers for claims from women for equal treatment. No doubt some employers have decided that it is best to wait until pressed by claims; some may believe that the claims will not be pressed.

(3) Concern about rising costs coupled with a fear that equal pay would increase still further the absenteeism of women, particularly those with domestic pressures demanding priority over regular attendance to perform relatively unskilled tasks.

150

(4) Reluctance to change traditional arrangements.

(5) Fear of consequential claims from men.

(6) Absence of job evaluation. In firms where the range of skills, knowledge and experience required is a wide one, the absence or otherwise of job evaluation will be a key factor determining the impact of the Act on the pay structure.

(7) Some of the key clauses in the Act are open to differing interpretations which will not be tested until the Industrial Tribunals hear claims in 1976.

(8) Discrimination between men and women in social insurance, taxation and employment conditions (the statutory restrictions).

(9) The lack of opportunity for women to enter the higher-paid fields of employment.

9 Experience overseas

European Economic Community [EEC]

In 1961 the Community adopted a three-year plan for implementation of equal pay as required by Article 119 of the Treaty of Rome which states:

Each member State shall in the course of the first stage ensure and subsequently maintain the application of the principle of equal remuneration for equal work as between men and women workers.

For the purposes of this article, remuneration shall mean the ordinary basic or minimum wage or salary, and any additional emoluments whatsoever, payable directly or indirectly, whether in cash or in kind, by the employer to the worker, and arising out of the worker's employment. Equal remuneration without discrimination based on sex means:

(a) that remuneration for the same work at piece-rates shall be calculated on the basis of the same unit of measurement and

(b) that remuneration for work at time rates shall be the same for the same job.

The lack of precision in this article has made it difficult for the EEC Commission to bring effective pressure on the six to ensure satisfactory progress, and at the end of 1961 the six Governments adopted a resolution setting out objectives for the three-year plan. The Government undertook:

to refuse to confer binding force on any collective agreement which, in spite of the instructions or recommendations of the Governments, do not ensure that the above time schedule :

respected (ie the elimination of discrimination in stages by the end of 1964) and acknowledged that . . .

the progressive application of the principle of equal pay for men and women aims at abolishing all discrimination in wages, and particularly:

   (i) fixing the minimum compulsory wage for men only, or fixing this minimum at a different level for men and women;
  (ii) fixing a different minimum compulsory wage for the two sexes when collective agreements, schedules or wage agreements provide for this;
 (iii) calculating the wage schedules for time-work and piece-work at a different rate for men and women;
  (iv) setting up different categories for men and women, or the use of different classification criteria when wages are fixed according to a system of job classification;
   (v) all other practices relating to collective agreements, schedules or wage agreements which maintain a difference in the wages earned by men and women."

The Governments also acknowledged that practices such as a systematic demotion of female workers, different rules of qualification for men and women, and the use of criteria based on the assessment of work for the classification of workers which has no bearing on the actual working conditions, are incompatible with the principle of equal pay for men and women.

In June 1970 the Commission submitted to the Council of Ministers its fifth report on implementation of the Article. The report dealt with the situation at the end of 1968. Lack of adequate data was evidently the main cause of delay in completing the report. The Commission reported that the six countries "were still far from having completely respected all the commitments entered upon". Some progress had been made on the legal and jurisdictional level, but there were still "inadequacies and even complete failure to act". Lack of progress was in part due to the absence of collective agreements for some sectors, direct discrimination (said to be very rare) or to indirect discrimination chiefly in connection with professional classification. Both sides of industry were urged to step up their efforts.

In July 1973 the Commission published its latest report, on developments up to the end of 1972. The Commission is still handicapped by the inadequacy of statistics but clearly came to the conclusion that the obligations imposed by the Treaty, and made more explicit by the 1961 Resolution, had still not been fully carried out. It seems that in the six countries, as in the UK, lack of agreement over the interpretation to be placed on the term equal work is a handicap to progress and no doubt most of the other obstacles referred to in chapter 8 are also present.

The Commission was able to report some progress, but warned member Governments that it would "start proceedings against certain (unspecified) Member States".

The Commission has pointed out that, unlike some other Clauses of the Rome Treaty, that concerning equal pay (Article 119) places a binding obligation on the Member States but is not directly applicable to individuals within those States. The EEC Court of Justice has ruled that provisions of the Treaty which contain precise, complete, obligations which exclude Member States from exercising discretion concerning them, can be invoked before a judge of the national court. The Commission points out that Convention 100 of the ILO has no more authority within any country which has ratified that Convention than Article 119 of the Rome Treaty.

In its report the Commission stated that it would be drafting a new community instrument which would clarify the "role and responsibilities of public authorities".

This draft was submitted to the Council of Ministers on 19 November 1973, as part of its Social Action Programme. The main points of the programme were accepted by the Council, but the Commission's timetable for action was significantly altered. The Council has undertaken to make a decision on the Commission's proposals within five months of receiving the opinions on them from the Economic and Social Committee and from the European Parliament. The Council will in any case make decisions within nine months. Included in the list for priority action is a draft directive on equal pay, as follows:

Article 1
This Directive is intended to approximate the laws, regulations and administrative provisions concerning the application of the principle that men and women should receive equal pay for equal work, contained in Article 119 of the Treaty establishing the European Economic Community and hereinafter called 'the principle of equal pay'.

Article 2
Member States shall introduce into their domestic legal systems such measures as are necessary to enable all persons who consider themselves aggrieved by the non-application of the principle of equal pay to enforce their claims before the courts.

Article 3
Member States shall abolish all discrimination between men and women arising from laws, regulations or administrative provisions affecting wages, particularly as regards the public and similar services, the legal minimum wage and statutory wage-related allowances or benefits other than those falling within social security systems which are directly regulated by law.

Article 4
Member States shall take all necessary measures to render ineffective any provisions contrary to the principle of equal pay which appear in collective agreements, wage scales, wage agreements or individual contracts of employment,

Article 5
Member States shall take the necessary measures to prevent any dismissals which might be construed as an employer's reaction to a complaint at the level of the undertaking or to suits tending to ensure that the principle of equal pay is respected.

Article 6
Member States shall ensure that the application of the

principle of equal pay is supervised at the level of the under-taking and that all infringements are punished.

Article 7
Provisions adopted in pursuance of this Directive and those already in force in this connection shall be brought to the attention of workers in any appropriate manner at their places of work.

Article 8
Within a period of six months, dating from the day that this Directive has been notified, the Member States shall amend their laws in accordance with the aforementioned minimal provisions and shall forthwith inform the Commission thereof. Laws thus amended shall enter into force one year after this Directive has been notified or not later than 31 December 1975.

Article 9
In the two years dating from the expiry of the period of one year specified in Article 8 and not later than 31 December 1977, the Member States shall forward to the Commission all the information enabling it to draw up a report on the applica-tion of this Directive for submission to the Council.

Furthermore, once this Directive has been notified, Member States shall ensure that the Commission is informed, in time for it to submit its comments, of the most important laws, regulations and administrative provisions which they envisage adopting in the field covered by this Directive.

Article 10
This Directive is addressed to the Member States.

Of particular interest to us in the UK is Article 6 because it would require the Government to ensure that any infringement of the principle of equal pay "at the level of the undertaking" is punished. The concept of punishment for the offender instead of compensation for the aggrieved party is a new departure.

The Council has also given approval to draft proposals designed to achieve some progress towards equal pay for men and women in employment. Under these proposals major priority is to be given to offering women oppor-

156

tunities of returning to work as soon as family responsibilities permit. The Commission proposes to set up a permanent working group on women's employment problems.

In its July 1973 report, the Commission also announced its intention to invite employers and unions to meet at a European level to negotiate a framework agreement prohibiting discriminatory collective agreements. The Commission proposes that the agreement should also lay down rules to ensure that job classification schemes are designed and applied as objectively as possible and that due weight is given to the characteristics that tend to be present more often in jobs performed by women than in those performed by men.

The Commission intends to put forward proposals for "the grading of the employment of women". The proposals will take account of the results of a study of women's employment in the EEC and of a sociological survey concerned with the general working conditions of women. A new study of the structure and distribution of wages in industry, commerce, banks and insurance is being carried out.

In its annual report for 1972 on social policy, the Commission stated:

> equal treatment will not really be possible until the fact of being a woman with special social responsibilities is no longer used as a pretext for inadequate training, interruption of professional careers, under-qualification and lesser chances of advancement. The development of appropriate legislation, taking into account the place of women in society, and the growth of collective facilities are closely linked with the chances of advancement of women at work.

Within the EEC the following moves are of special interest:

Germany

There has been a good deal of publicity about alleged discrimination against women in certain industries where, it is said, undue weight has been given to the physical effort required in tasks commonly performed by men. In its report on the position in 1966, the EEC Commission lent support to the views of German trade unions on the matter and its latest proposal concerning job classification is, no doubt, directed specifically at the industries concerned. In practice, it seems that few cases have come before the labour courts which have powers to deal with them. This may well be because in Germany no administrative checks are provided by legislation.

It seems that some movement away from the present segregation of 'light work' and 'heavy work' may have started. Incomes Data Services reported (Study No 56) in July 1973 that, in the collective agreement for the engineering industry in the Nordrhein Westfalen region, effective from January 1973, the 'light work' category has been abolished and those affected moved up from wage group I to wage group II.

Denmark

An all-industry national agreement between the Danish Employers' Association and the Trade Union Federation came into effect on 28 March 1973. This agreement confirmed an earlier understanding that equal pay should be introduced by the mid-year; accordingly time rates were to be unified by 10 April and piece rates by 1 July. In some industries these requirements had already been negotiated in anticipation of the national agreement.

France

The 1946 Constitution recognized the right of women to equality with men in all spheres and this was confirmed in the 1958 Constitution. A decree of July 1946 prohibited different basic wage rates for men and women in collective agreements and a further statute passed in February 1950 required that collective agreements should be in accord with the principle of equal pay for equal work. Under this law, employees may seek to secure their rights through the civil courts or through local tribunals. In December 1972 a new law requiring equal pay for work of equal value (in accordance with ILO Convention 100) was introduced. Inspectors are empowered to make investigations and to hold enquiries. However, the Commission has received reports from French trade unions to the effect that the number of inspectors is insufficient to deal with the "mass of tasks they must accomplish".

Ireland

In December 1972 a Commission on the Status of Women published its report. As yet, a promise that the Commission's findings would be incorporated in an Equal Pay Bill has not been implemented. Some progress has been made through National Agreements. The 1972 agreement provided for claims for narrowing or eliminating differences in the rate of pay for men and women in any of the following circumstances:

(a) where women are performing the same jobs as men or where men and women are completely interchangeable between jobs;
(b) where the jobs performed by men and women are of a similar nature but contain difference which occur only infrequently or are of small practical importance in relation to total job content;
(c) where it is established that the jobs performed by men and women are of equal value in that the demands (for instance in relation to skill, physical or mental effort, responsibility and working conditions) made on a woman are equal to the demands made on a man in respect of the work each performs;
(d) where pay is differentiated on a marriage basis.

Disputes arising from such claims can be referred to a Labour Court with a request to appoint an Equal Pay Commissioner to investigate the claim and report to the Court and the parties. If need be, the Court can make a final decision on the claim. The trade unions undertook to "cooperate fully in the use of job evaluation or other techniques for the purpose of establishing the validity of a claim". Where the claim for equal pay is declared valid, the differential could be reduced by 17 per cent. The 1974 agreement provides for the gap to be reduced by one-third. Unlike the UK's Equal Pay Act, the agreement makes no provision for the elimination of women's rates as such from collective agreements.

The only claim under this agreement so far adjudicated on by a Labour Court Commissioner was rejected on the ground that, because it was an industry-wide claim (covering women confectioners) any decision would have to apply throughout the industry, and the Commissioner was not satisfied that the jobs being performed would meet the criteria laid down in the National Agreement in every case.

Netherlands

There is no legal or statutory provision for bringing the principle of equal pay into effect. However, ILO Convention 100 was ratified in 1972. The Netherlands is the only one of the six member countries covered by the Commission's report where the Government has power to cancel a discriminatory collective agreement. On the other hand, it is the only country, according to the Commission's report, which has not implemented the 1961 commitment to refuse to confer binding force on any collective agreements which did not meet the agreed timetable for ending discrimination.

The Commission believes that it is mainly through collective agreements that progress towards equal pay will be achieved, and has therefore expressed concern about the proportion of the working population in the Netherlands not covered by such an agreement or wage regulation. The Commission reported that at the end of 1972 between 20 per cent and 25 per cent were not covered, as compared with 17 per cent in 1964. But the Commission has reported more favourably on the use of job classification systems in the Netherlands. Such systems are said to be based on job evaluation, and the criteria used are "objective and independent of the sex of the worker".

United States

The Equal Pay Act of 1963 amended the Fair Labor Standards Act of 1938 to require the men and women within an establishment performing "equal work on jobs that require equal skill, effort and responsibility, and which are performed under similar working conditions" are paid "equal wage rates", except where "such payment is made pursuant to (i) a seniority system; (ii) a merit system; (iii) a system which measures earnings by quantity or quality of production; or (iv) a differential based on any other factor other than sex".

These requirements apply to employees engaged in inter-state commerce, or in the production of goods for inter-state commerce, and to other employees in certain enterprises so engaged. Thus the Act covers a wide field of employment. It is enforced by the Wages and Hours Division of the Federal Department of Labour. In response to a question from the Select Committee, Mrs Catherine East, Executive Secretary, Citizens' Advisory Council on Status of Women, said that the extent to which equal pay had been achieved was not known. Only the last year or so had definitive court decisions been made and some employers are becoming concerned about the prospect of successful claims for back pay. Such evidence as one can gather suggests that as yet the Act has had relatively little impact on women's wage levels.

The American experience in legislation aimed at widening the opportunities for women is of considerable interest at this time. Title VII of the Civil Rights Act, which came into effect in July 1965, prohibits discrimination, by employers, labour unions and employment agencies, based on race, colour, religion, sex and national origin. It covers employers with 15 or more employees and unions with 15 or more members. Title VII was amended in 1972, by the Equal Employment Opportunities Act, to give more enforcement powers, including the right of the Equal Employment Opportunities Commission [EEOC] to sue in a Federal Court.

The machinery of EEOC is set in motion by an aggrieved person, or one of the five Commissioners, filing a charge at a 'field office'. A decision may be made at local or federal level. If the charge is found to be invalid, the aggrieved person has the right to institute proceedings at a federal court. If the EEOC finds reasonable cause to believe that the Act has been violated, it will attempt to secure conciliation and, if this is unsuccessful, the EEOC can institute proceedings in a Federal Court. The US Attorney General also has the right to institute proceedings. Back pay liability, in the event of a reinstatement being endorsed, may be up to two years before the filing of the charge with the EEOC. Section 1604.1 of Title VII states:

(1) The Commission will find that the following situations do not warrant the application of the *bona fide* occupational qualification exception:
> (i) The refusal to hire a woman because of her sex, based on assumptions of the comparative employment characteristics of women in general, For example, the assumption that the turnover rate among women is higher than among men.
> (ii) The refusal to hire an individual based on stereo-typed characterizations of the sexes. Such stereotypes include, for example, that men are less capable of assembling intricate equipment; that women are less capable of aggressive salesmanship. The principle of non-discrimination requires that individuals be considered on the basis of individual capacities and not on the basis of any characteristics generally attributed to the group.
> (iii) The refusal to hire an individual because of the preferences of co-workers, the employer, clients or customers except as covered specifically in sub-paragraph (2) of this paragraph.

    (iv) The fact that the employer may have to provide separate facilities for a person of the opposite sex will not justify discrimination under the *bona fide* occupational qualification exception unless the expense would clearly be unreasonable.

(2) Where it is necessary for the purpose of authenticity or genuineness, the Commission will consider sex to be a *bona fide* occupational qualification, eg an actor or actress.

(To the end of 1972 the only jobs for which sex has been accepted by the courts as a *bona fide* occupational qualification are actor, actress and wet-nurse.)

Section 1604.2 states:

(a) It is an unlawful employment practice to classify a job as 'male' or 'female' or to maintain separate lines of progression or separate seniority lists based on sex where this would adversely affect any employee unless sex is a *bona fide* occupational qualification for that job. Accordingly employment practices are unlawful which arbitrarily classify jobs so that:

    (1) A female is prohibited from applying for a job labelled 'male', or for a job in a 'male' line of progression; and *vice versa*.

    (2) A male scheduled for layoff is prohibited from displacing a less senior female on a 'female' seniority list; and *vice versa*.

(b) A seniority system or line of progression which distinguishes between 'light' and 'heavy' jobs constitutes an unlawful employment practice if it operates as a disguised form of classification by sex, or creates unreasonable obstacles to the advancement of members of either sex into jobs which members of that sex would reasonably be expected to perform."

Section 1604.3 prohibits a marriage bar except where it applies equally to men and women.

In an article published by *Industrial Relations Review and Report* (No 63, September 1973), Debby King, Research Officer of a leading American Trade Union, stated that it takes an average of two years for complaints to be processed by the EEOC and longer still if the case has to be referred to the Courts. She thought that progress had also been slow because the legislation was not the result of pressure from women. It had been "practically ignored by the press". The same point was made by Mrs Sonia Pressman Fuentes, Chief of the Legislative Counsel Division of the General Counsel's Office at the EEOC; in her evidence to the Select Committee she said:

> "Until the passage of legislation prohibiting sex discrimination in the United States, the overwhelming majority of our people – women as well as men – were not aware that women had second-class status in our society . . . it was the passage of legislation prohibiting sex discrimination that led to the current women's rights movement in the United States."
>
> SBN 401373 p 128

It seems, therefore, that a few more years must pass before very much can be learned from the US experience.

10 Action points
Equal Pay Act, 1970

There is an urgent need for a more general and much fuller awareness of the roles that women are playing in our society. The need is urgent because children (both girls and boys) are being subjected to a conditioning which severely restricts their freedom of choice in education, training and employment.

Women can no longer be treated as a reserve of labour to be drawn on only when expedient. The community's standard of living depends on the efforts of men and women, and all should have an equal opportunity to choose and train for a career (not merely an occupation).

Adequate provision should be made for career guidance in schools – guidance which takes account of possible future roles and anticipates the probable return of girls to employment, if they intend first to bring up a family.

Complacency about the educational provisions for girls must be challenged. Discrimination is severely restricting their development and helping to maintain the present narrow choice in employment. Differences in the standard of facilities in science and in the opportunities for studying mathematics cannot be accepted as sensible or fair.

Everybody concerned with the provision and use of training opportunities and further education should take deliberate steps to see that the opportunities for girls and women are enlarged. In particular more girls should be accepted for sandwich courses and day release, and advanced courses in further education should be offered to many more girls.

The discrimination against married women in education and training grants should be ended.

Exemption from training levy should only be granted where the Manpower Services Commission and the Training Services Agency are satisfied that reasonable progress in widening the opportunities for girls and women is being achieved. Industrial Training Boards should, with the help of the Training Services Agency, examine all the jobs in their industry, listing those where women could be employed. Consideration should also be given to special grants for firms which train girls and women for jobs outside the traditional range of women's work and to firms which provide re-training and promotion opportunities for women returning to employment.

The number of Government Training Centres should be increased, the range of occupations for which training is provided should be widened and part-time training should be offered wherever practicable. Industrial Training Boards and Government Training Centres should be organized to collect and publish data on the sex of trainees and the jobs for which they are being trained. Current assumptions about the aptitudes and interests of women must be challenged and more opportunities to train for a career in, for example, industrial management, scientific research, applied mathematics, should be offered.

Similar re-examination is needed with regard to the opportunities for men in, for example, nursing.

The vicious circle of few candidates, therefore few vacancies offered, therefore few trained, therefore few candidates . . . must be broken. Action is needed at all three points. Training opportunities must be widened; women must be encouraged to apply for positions from which they have generally been excluded and employers must be persuaded to consider women candidates equally with men. Persuasion alone is unlikely to achieve much change. Legislation is urgently needed to back up and stimulate the process of persuasion and education.

Professional bodies generally could do much more to promote change through seminars and conferences and through offering advice to employers and their members about the changes needed. They could examine the reasons for the exclusion of women from their professions, or the handicaps that women have to overcome to gain entry and consider what changes would help to facilitate their entry and their effective employment in the profession. The IPM, for example, could investigate the personal aptitudes and training needed for effective work in the industrial relations field of personnel management with a view to encouraging more women to seek a full career in the profession.

The criteria for appointments to public boards should be broadened and more regard paid to the contribution that women as full partners in the economic life of the community, as well as consumers, can make.

The segregation of jobs into men's work and women's work is wasteful of talents and potential skills, leads to frustration and resentment from those who long for a wider choice, and is uneconomic since it inevitably increases the number of pressure points in the labour market. A continuing effort to widen the range of work open to both men and women can make a significant contribution to overall effectiveness.

Conditions of employment generally have been designed to attract and retain men. They are not as suitable for married women and adaptation is long overdue in many firms. Part-time work, and the conditions associated with part-time work, flexible working hours, special leave arrangements, sick pay and maternity leave, need to be considered in the light of the increasing employment of women (see chapter 6 for a discussion of these matters).

167

Proposals for a "code of sound practices in the field of employment of women" should be resisted. A more helpful approach might be to offer, where the work permits, a less demanding contract for those women (and men) that are unable to take employment involving all the normal pressures for regular attendance (see page 75).

Local authorities should be required to provide sufficient play centres and nurseries to meet the needs of parents and their children.

Discrimination in taxation, social insurance, retirement, pensions, facilities for finance and ownership of property should be removed. Family allowances should be raised at least sufficiently to take account of inflation since the last increase. A loss of income allowance should replace the maternity allowance and be paid to an expectant mother for such period as is generally felt to be required to enable the mother to free herself for re-entry to employment (see page 80).

Where the range of skills, knowledge and experience required for the various jobs performed is wide, job evaluation should be considered. A joint employer/trade union investigation of the problems and needs in evaluating work could provide an enduring basis for determining the basis for implementing equal pay and may also make it easier for trade unions to cooperate in a review of employment opportunities. Legislation covering Equal Pay and Equal Opportunity should come into effect at the same time (see also the IPM statements in chapter 1 for comments on the Government proposals for legislation and other views).

Appendix 1

Female activity rates: historical and projected

		1951	1961	1971	1981	1986
16–19*	Married females	38·1	41·1	42·4	42·4	42·4
	Other females	96·1	97·7	97·7	97·7	97·7
20–24*	Married females	36·6	41·4	46·7	48·7	48·7
	Other females	94·3	95·3	94·4	94·4	94·4
25–34	Married females	24·4	29·5	38·4	41·7	43·3
	Other females	85·1	87·9	80·8	78·0	76·6
35–44	Married females	25·7	36·4	54·5	63·3	66·4
	Other females	77·0	81·7	80·0	78·8	78·2
45–54	Married females	23·7	35·3	57·0	68·2	73·2
	Other females	67·2	75·5	78·1	78·0	77·9
55–59	Married females	15·6	26·0	45·5	56·5	60·5
	Other females	50·9	63·1	67·2	65·9	65·3
60–64	Married females	7·2	12·7	25·2	31·6	33·2
	Other females	25·2	32·3	33·7	31·2	30·0
65+	Married females	2·7	3·4	6·5	8·5	9·5
	Other females	6·4	6·9	6·3	6·1	6·0

NOTE: All historical activity rates are based on Census of Population data
* Includes students as economically active.

Source: Department of Employment *Gazette,* February, 1974

Appendix 2

Courses of study provided by schools, January, 1972

(PERCENTAGES OF SCHOOLS)

			Percentage of Schools Providing Courses:				
CATEGORY OF SCHOOL		Total Number of Schools	Beyond 'A' Level	'A' Level	Beyond 'O' Level or CSE (But Below 'A' Level)	'O' Level or CSE	No GCE or C... with Pupils Aged 15 on 31/8/71
MAINTAINED SCHOOLS							
Modern	Boys	326	Nil	21·2	2·1	97·0	1·5
,,	Girls	343	Nil	23·4	3·2	98·0	0·6
,,	Mixed	1,549	0·1	17·9	1·9	96·5	0·9
Grammar	Boys	299	25·0	100·0	7·0	100·0	Nil
,,	Girls	322	3·1	99·4	24·6	100·0	Nil
,,	Mixed	272	7·0	99·6	8·1	99·6	Nil
Comprehensive	Boys	133	6·8	74·4	0·8	94·0	Nil
,,	Girls	131	2·3	72·5	19·1	94·7	Nil
,,	Mixed	1,327	2·8	63·3	7·0	88·5	0·8
Technical and Other Secondary	Boys	78	2·6	87·3	5·1	98·7	Nil
,,	Girls	57	Nil	77·2	26·4	100·0	Nil
,,	Mixed	189	1·1	57·2	10·0	97·3	Nil
All Middle	Boys	7	Nil	Nil	Nil	Nil	Nil
,, ,,	Girls	8	Nil	Nil	Nil	Nil	Nil
,, ,,	Mixed	308	Nil	0·3	Nil	2·3	0·3
DIRECT GRANT GRAMMAR SCHOOLS							
	Boys	80	37·5	100·0	11·2	100·0	Nil
	Girls	94	5·4	100·0	26·6	100·0	Nil
	Mixed	2	(1 only)	(2 only)	Nil	(2 only)	Nil
INDEPENDENT SECONDARY AND PRIMARY/SECONDARY*							
	Boys	241	16·6	82·2	6·6	95·0	5·0
	Girls	325	1·5	86·8	28·0	90·8	9·2
	Mixed	110	0·9	57·3	3·6	76·4	23·6
ALL SCHOOLS							
	Boys	1,164	13·4	69·8	5·0	96·7	1·5
	Girls	1,280	1·8	71·5	19·2	98·0	0·4
	Mixed	3,757	1·7	41·6	4·5	85·6	1·4
Total		6,201	3·9	53·1	7·6	90·3	1·2
Total Numbers		—	(241)	(3,290)	(470)	(5,599)	(73)

* Recognized as efficient.
Source: Statistics of Education, 1972 Vol 1, (E & W).

ppendix 3

rses followed by older pupils, January, 1972.
centages of those following an 'A' level course)

Category of School	Number of pupils following GCE 'A' Level Courses		Percentage on courses including subjects in the Maths/Science group		Percentage on courses which include Maths	
	Boys	Girls	Boys	Girls	Boys	Girls
ntained schools						
dern	3,150	2,977	52.2	20.1	29.2	4.5
mmar	54,284	51,382	64.9	38.1	47.6	19.0
hnical	2,987	1,714	70.5	35.5	53.7	14.5
nprehensive	45,514	37,701	65.0	32.2	42.7	14.0
er	4,295	3,477	60.9	30.0	41.7	14.0
ct Grant Grammar chools	12,468	11,424	61.2	41.1	46.3	21.5
pendent Schools*	22,288	12,108	55.4	35.0	34.6	13.0
the above schools	144,986	120,783	62.9	35.5	43.5	16.5

ls' percentages as percentage of boys' percentages

	Percentages on courses which include	
	Maths and subjects in the Science group†	Mathematics
intained Schools		
dern	38.5	15.4
mmar	58.7	40.0
hnical	50.4	27.0
nprehensive	49.5	32.8
er	49.3	33.6
ct Grant Grammar	67.1	46.5
ependent Schools*	63.3	37.5
the above	56.4	38.0

ecognized as efficient.
Physics, Chemistry, Botany Biology, Zoology, Geology, Technical Drawing, lding Construction, Metal Work, Woodwork, Engineering Science.

rce: Statistics of Education, 1972, Vol 1 (England and Wales).

Appendix 4

Qualifications and destination of pupils leaving school during the academic year 1970-71 (England, Wales and N. Ireland)*

Level of qualification held on leaving School	Number holding qualification (000s)	Destination (percentages)			
		University	College of Education	Further Education	Employment
1 to 4 'O' levels (No 'A')					
Boys	58·28	<0·1	0·2	16·4	83·4
Girls	58·54	<0·1	0·4	25·4	74·2
5 or more 'O' levels (No 'A')					
Boys	22·27	0·2	3·8	22·7	73·3
Girls	28·88	0·1	11·7	30·5	57·8
1—'A' level					
Boys	11·59	1·1	12·2	29·5	57·2
Girls	11·03	0·7	40·0	21·0	38·3
2—'A' levels					
Boys	15·49	20·8	8·5	33·0	37·7
Girls	15·20	11·3	35·9	25·3	27·5
3 or more 'A' levels					
Boys	31·67	68·2	2·4	13·0	16·4
Girls	22·04	57·7	13·7	14·3	14·3

*Information covering Scotland is not available for 1970–71.
†Including those leaving for temporary employment pending entry to Further (Part time) Education and with destination not known.

Source: Education Statistics for the UK, 1971.

Destination on leaving school related to type of school, 1971. (England and Wales)

Percentages

Destination	Maintained Schools all maintained Boys	Girls	Grammar only Boys	Girls	Direct Grant Schools Boys	Girls	Independent Schools* Boys	Girls
Universities	5·7	3·5	23·7	14·2	39·3	29·1	27·4	14·7
Colleges of Education	1·3	4·9	4·1	16·2	3·3	15·8	1·0	6·9
Polytechnics	2·1	1·1	6·7	3·8	7·7	3·4	5·0	2·1
Other Full-time Further Education	7·4	11·9	10·6	18·7	13·1	18·0	24·2	38·8
Employment†	83·6	78·6	54·9	47·1	36·5	33·6	42·3	37·5
Total	100·0	100·0	100·0	100·0	100·0	100·0	100·0	100·0
Leavers (000s)	(292·8)	(279·2)	(45·6)	(47·7)	(7·8)	(7·6)	(14·8)	(11·2)

Percentages going to University or College of Education

Category of School	University Boys	Girls	College of Education Boys	Girls	University or College of Education Boys	Girls
All Maintained	5·7	3·5	1·3	4·9	7·0	8·4
Maintained Grammar	23·7	14·2	4·1	16·2	27·8	30·4
Direct Grant	39·3	29·1	3·3	15·8	42·6	44·9
Independent*	27·4	14·7	1·0	6·9	28·4	21·6
Total	7·5	4·6	1·3	5·2	8·8	9·8

*Recognized as efficient (excluding Special Schools).
†Including temporary employment pending entry to Full-time Further Education, other destinations and destination not known.

Source: Statistics of Education, 1971, Vol 2 (England and Wales).

Appendix 6

Results achieved by students holding full value awards which terminated in calendar year 1971

	Successes		Premature terminations				Final examination failure		Unknown		Total	
			Examination failure		Other reasons							
	Men	Women	Men	Women	Men	Women	Men	Women	Men	Women	Men	Women
England and Wales Universities												
Undergraduate and non-graduate courses												
First degree courses*	26,509	11,605	1,969	429	1,602	847	638	151	716	232	31,434	13,264
Diploma or certificate courses	98	40	2	—	—	—	3	2	10	1	113	43
Other courses†	92	94	2	—	—	5	5	—	6	2	105	101
Postgraduate courses	45	22	1	—	2	—	—	1	3	1	51	24
All university courses	26,744	11,761	1,974	429	1,604	852	646	154	735	236	31,703	13,432
Further education establishments												
Undergraduate and non-graduate courses												
First degree courses	4,284	1,277	1,163	200	777	327	400	157	278	58	6,902	2,019
Comparable courses‡	1,894	1,133	209	66	261	168	165	55	159	64	2,688	1,486
HND courses	3,474	600	649	92	575	176	500	87	220	65	5,418	1,020
Other courses†	9,910	7,701	482	209	1,115	1,023	1,263	625	915	637	13,685	10,195
Postgraduate courses	516	361	3	1	27	20	129	32	50	51	725	465
All further education courses	20,078	11,072	2,506	568	2,755	1,714	2,457	956	1,622	875	29,418	15,185

*Including further first degree courses. The figures for first degree courses at further education establishments include courses for CNAA awards. Successes in first degree courses at all establishments include pass degrees courses and students obtaining aegrotat degrees (awarded to students who are prevented by illness or other sufficient reason from completing their final examination).

†Including courses for which there is no final examination or qualification.

‡See paragraph 3 of the Explanatory Notes

Numbers

Degrees obtained in 1969-70 (UK)

SUBJECT	First Degrees						Higher Degrees					
	Pass or Ordinary		Honours		Total		Doctorates		Others		Total	
	Men	Women	Men	Women	Men	Women	Men	Women	Men	Women	Men	Women
Education	306	342	263	309	569	651	28	5	354	67	382	66
Medicine, Dentistry and Health	2,232	675	568	314	2,800	989	428	75	160	48	588	123
Engineering and Technology	1,692	18	6,020	89	7,712	107	939	6	1,589	24	2,528	30
Agriculture, Forestry and Veterinary Science	291	54	372	90	663	144	169	13	176	24	345	37
Science	1,460	585	7,778	2,645	9,238	3,230	2,338	210	1,306	219	3,644	429
(Included in Science)												
Mathematics	319	106	1,552	546	1,871	652	243	10	390	71	633	81
Physics	205	41	1,493	237	1,698	278	486	20	258	32	744	52
Chemistry	280	42	1,926	299	2,206	341	932	55	257	22	1,189	77
Social Administration and Business Studies	922	432	6,550	3,064	7,472	3,496	348	46	1,458	280	1,806	326
(Included in SA and BS)												
Economics	154	25	1,124	193	1,278	218	73	6	300	37	373	43
Law	281	50	1,222	269	1,503	319	36	1	198	22	234	23
Psychology	13	6	361	392	374	398	63	17	61	32	124	49
Sociology	18	25	433	642	451	667	34	5	147	72	181	77
Architecture and other Professional and Vocational Subjects	107	26	462	77	569	103	22	—	317	55	339	55
(Included in Architecture etc.)												
Home, Hotel and Institutional Management	28	20	—	1	28	21	—	—	3	—	3	—
Language Literature and Area Studies	72	146	2,698	3,423	2,770	3,569	188	58	428	215	616	273
Arts (other than Languages)	636	1,115	1,853	1,418	2,489	2,533	228	29	292	87	520	116
All Subjects	7,718	3,393	26,564	11,429	34,282	14,822	4,688	442	6,080	1,013	10,768	1,455

Source: Statistics of Education, 1970, Vol 6 (Universities).

Appendix 8

Number of First Class Honours Degrees as percentage of all Honours Degrees

Subject	Men	Women	Tot
Education	0·8	0·3	0·
Medicine, Dentistry and Health	7·6	9·2	8·
Engineering and Technology	12·3	15·7	12·
Agriculture, Forestry and Veterinary Science	7·3	5·6	6·
Science	14·5	10·1	13·
(Included in Science)			
Mathematics	18·1	12·8	16·
Physics	16·5	12·7	16·
Chemistry	14·2	14·3	14·
Social Administration and Business Studies	4·2	2·8	3·
(Included in SA and BS)			
Economics	3·2	2·1	3·
Law	4·3	5·6	4·
Psychology	6·6	4·9	5·
Sociology	3·2	3·0	3·
Architecture and other Professional and Vocational Subjects	13·6	3·9	12·
Language, Literature and Area Studies	8·3	5·1	6·
Arts, (other than Languages)	7·6	3·4	5·
All Subjects	10·0	5·5	8·

*Only 3 awarded with First Class Honours.

Source: Statistics of Education, 1970, Vol 6 (Universities).

Appendix 9

DAY AND BLOCK RELEASE COURSES
Numbers released by employer in November 1971 as percentage of numbers insured at June 1971

| | | *Percentages* |
| | | |
Industry	*Men*	*Women*
Food, drink and tobacco	15·8	5·2
Chemicals and allied	52·3	15·0
Metal manufacturing	69·4	39·3
Mechanical engineering	74·9	22·3
Instrument engineering	33·3	7·8
Electrical engineering	82·9	7·0
Vehicles	59·8	18·3
Metal goods (n.c.s.)	18·5	9·1
Textiles	9·1	3·6
Clothing and footwear	10·4	2·0
Bricks, pottery, glass and cement	16·9	9·9
Timber, furniture	22·5	3·9
Paper, printing and publishing	38·3	4·1
Other manufacturing	21·8	6·0
Total (including non-manufacturing and services)	35·9	9·6

Source: Statistics of Education, 1971, Vol 3 (Further Education)

Appendix 10

**Further education (public sector and assisted sector)
Number of students, Autumn 1971.**

Thous‸

Mode of attendance	Age 15 to 20 inclusive		Age 21 and over		Age 15 and ov‸	
	Males	Females	Males	Females	Males	Fem‸
Full-time (excluding Short Courses)	106·8	103·0	39·2	18·3	146·0	12‸
Short Full-time	4·0	0·8	7·8	2·1	11·8	‸
Sandwich	19·8	3·7	18·0	1·1	37·8	‸
Part time Day	437·7	94·5	156·9	109·5	594·6	20‸
Evening	273·1	281·3	586·0	1,188·7	859·1	1,46‸
Total	841·4	483·3	807·9	1,319·7	1,649·3	1 80‸

Number of female students as percentage of total students

Percent‸

Mode of Attendance	Age 15 to 20 inclusive	Age 21 and over	Age 15 an‸ over
Full-time (excluding Short Courses)	49·1	31·8	45·4
Short Full-time	17·1	21·1	19·8
Sandwich	15·9	5·8	11·4
Part-time Day	17·7	41·0	25·5
Evening	50·8	67·0	63·1
Total	36·4	62·0	52·2

Further education students taking advanced courses leading to recognized qualifications

Thousa‸

Level of Qualification	Full-time		Sandwich		Part-time Day		Evening	
	Males	Females	Males	Females	Males	Females	Males	Fema‸
University Degree, CNAA Degree and Diplomas of SCI*	17·0	8·0	15·7	1·6	1·9	0·3	2·0	0‸
HND and HNC	6·3	2·1	12·5	1·4	33·1	3·1	5·5	0·‸
Others	22·1	13·7	3·2	0·3	34·5	4·1	28·6	3·‸
Total	45·4	23·8	31·4	3·3	69·5	7·5	36·1	4·‸

*Scottish Central Institutions.

Source: Education Statistics for the UK, 1971.

ppendix 11

entage increase in numbers of GCE passes between 1960 and 1970
nber of passes in 1970 in brackets)

	Maths	Physics	Chemistry	Economics	English Language	English Literature	All Subjects
vels							
	24·1 (101,557)	46·1 (47,846)	34·6 (36,156)	254·1 (20,852)	28·7 (94,074)	36·1 (52,104)	34·7 (669,580)
	61·1 (56,053)	119·4 (11,997)	137·4 (14,711)	378·2 (14,508)	65·0 (112,950)	46·6 (82,945)	52·3 (656,239)
	35·1	56·5	53·8	296·3	46·2	42·3	42·9
	(157,610)	(59,843)	(50,867)	(35,360)	(206,664)	(135,049)	(1,325,819)
evels							
	49·7 (34,866)	29·7 (23,350)	15·9 (16,136)	311·9 (19,659)	— —	147·4 (15,041)	79·5 (180,673)
	141·0 (8,603)	86·6 (4,684)	97·2 (5,301)	653·4 (6,042)	—	210·3 (26,331)	168·2 (122,653)
	61·8 (43,469)	36·6 (28,034)	29·1 (21,437)	361·0 (25,701)	—	184·1 (41,372)	107·2 (303,326)

e: SBN 416072, p23.

Appendix 12

Change in numbers of men and women entering higher education from 1961 to 1970

	Men			Women		
	1961 (000s)	1970 (000s)	*Percent increase*	1961 (000s)	1970 (000s)	*Percent increase*
Colleges of Education (England and Wales)	4·8	9·6	100	11·5	26·2	128
Advanced Further Education (England and Wales)	7·5	23·3	210	2·0	8·0	400
Universities (GB)	25·8	42·4	65	9·5	19·9	110
Total	38·1	75·3	97	23·0	54·1	135

Source: SBN 416072 p 25.

Appendix 13

Number of women in some Civil Service
Departmental Executive Grades, January 1972

Class and Grade	Total employed*	Women as percentage
Information Officer Class		
Chief Information Officer (A)	33	Nil
Chief Information Officer (B)	29	6·9
Principal Information Officer	112	10·7
Senior Information Officer	256·5	16·6
Information Officer	571	20·1
Assistant Information Officer	329	38·9
Total	1,330·5	22·5
Inland Revenue, Collection Service		
Principal Collector	20	Nil
Regional Collector	56	Nil
Senior Collector	172	9·3
Collector HG	222	12·2
Collector	658	25·4
Total	1,128	18·6
Inland Revenue, Inspectors Branch		
Chief or Deputy Chief Inspector	3	Nil
Senior Principal Inspector	36	Nil
Principal Inspector	319	0·3
Senior Inspector	617	2·4
Inspector HG	1,041	6·1
Inspector	3,253	10·8
Total	5,269	8·2
Department of Employment		
Grade 1	28	10·7
Grade 2	157	13·4
Grade 3	555	11·5
Grade 4	1,414	15·2
Grade 5	5,078	28·7
Cadets	29	31·0
Total	7,261	24·4
Exchequer and Audit		
Deputy Secretary and Secretary	3	Nil
Director of Audit	17	Nil
Deputy Director	77	1·3
Chief Auditor	243	8·2
Auditor	164·5	9·1
Assistant Auditor	467	18·8
Total	971·5	12·4

Part-time employees counted as halves.
Source: SBN 416072, p72–74.

Appendix 14

Occupational analysis from population census reports* for 1961, 1966 and 19
Females as percentage of total number in each occupation.

Occupation	1961	1966	1971
Administrators and Managers			
Ministers of the Crown, MP's and Senior Government Officials	11·5	11·3	11·3
Local authority Senior Officials	11·6	15·4	17·3
Managers in: Engineering and Allied Trades	2·6	3·0	3·1
Building and Contracting	3·1	4·0	3·6
Mining and Production (nec)	7·4	7·4	7·3
Personnel Managers	27·0	28·2	25·0
Sales Managers	2·0	3·5	3·9
Company Directors	15·9	20·9	†
Manager (nec)	6·9	9·1	11·4
Total (Administrators and Managers)	6·3	7·4	8·4
Professional, Technical Workers, Artists			
Medical Practitioners (qualified)	16·0	18·0	17·9
Dental Practitioners	6·6	10·6	19·0
Nurses	90·1	91·2	91·3
Pharmacists (and Dispensers in 1961 and 1966)	31·9	33·0	22·8
Radiographers (Medical and Industrial)	71·4	66·7	73·0
Opthalmic and Dispensing Opticians	—	—	19·7
Chiropodists and Physiotherapists	—	—	80·6
Public Health Inspectors	—	—	7·7
University Teachers	13·2	13·1	13·5
Teachers (nec)	59·2	58·3	57·6
Engineers (Civil, Structural, Municipal, Mechanical, Electrical, Electronic)	0·2	0·4	0·7
Chemists, Physical and Biological Scientists	7·0	7·3	9·0
Technologists, Technical and Related Workers	2·6	4·3	5·7
Professional Workers (nec)	35·9	32·9	39·8
Medical Workers (nec)	46·4	49·4	68·4
Laboratory Assistants, Technicians	32·3	35·0	38·8
Draughtsmen	10·0	10·4	10·5
Occupational Therapists	—	—	96·8
Social Welfare and Related Workers	47·3	52·2	61·8
Clergy, Ministers, Members of Religious Orders	23·6	22·8	16·8
Authors, Journalists and Related Workers	20·0	23·1	21·5
Stage Managers, Actors, Entertainers and Musicians	33·6	34·5	30·3
Painters, Sculptors and Related Workers	36·0	35·9	42·8
Accountants, Company Secretaries and Registrars	13·2	14·5	17·0
Surveyors, Architects (and Town Planners in 1971)	2·2	1·9	1·7
Judges, Barristers, Advocates, Solicitors	3·9	5·0	4·3
Total (Professional, Technical Workers, Artists)	38·1	38·3	38·5

*From 10 per cent sample tables in 1961 and 1966 and 1 per cent tables in 1971.
nec—Not elsewhere classified.
†Not classified in 1971.

182

Full-time teachers in the Public sector and assisted establishments, 1970-71 (provisional)

Category of School	Graduates		Non-graduates		Total	
	Total Number	Women as percent.	Total Number	Women as percent.	Total Number	Women as percent.
Public Sector						
Primary	13,688	59·5	188,559	77·9	202·247	76·8
Secondary	76,718	38·3	121,507	46·2	198,225	42·8
Assisted and Public Sector						
Special Schools	1,110	56·4	9,094	58·0	10,204	57·5
Colleges of Education	6,918	25·5	5,148	44·0	12,066	33·4
Other Education Establishments	20,467	13·9	38,361	15·7	58·828	15·1
Assisted Grammar	6,786	41·7	3,301	62·7	10,087	45·1
Miscellaneous	725	30·5	2,117	35·5	2,842	34·4
Total	126,412	35·7	368,087	59·7	494,499	53·5

Percentages of full-time women teachers that are married, 1970-71 (provisional.)

Category of School	Graduates	Non-graduates	Total
England and Wales			
Primary	41·2	49·1	48·7
Secondary	19·0	24·7	22·7
Scotland			
Primary	31·4	51·5	47·1
Secondary	18·6	23·2	20·5
Ireland			
Primary	20·2	46·7	45·0
Secondary	21·9	23·1	22·6

Source: Education Statistics for the UK 1971

Appendix 16

Grade of teachers* in Maintained Schools at 31st March, 1971 (provisional)
Number of women as percentage of total in each grade.

Percentage

Grade	Primary† Schools	Secondary Schools				
		Modern	Grammar	Technical	Compre-hensive	All Sections
Head Teachers						
Graduates	21·3	9·2	35·7	14·3	10·8	16·9
Total	43·2	17·6	36·4	14·7	13·6	20·8
Deputy Head (also Department Head)						
Graduates	40·0‡	21·4	41·6	30·8	19·3	32·2
Total	51·4	29·4	42·2	33·3	27·3	34·0
Deputy Head (not Department Head)						
Graduates	39·0	22·6	44·3	31·0	26·6	31·5
Total	60·5	35·4	46·0	27·8	33·8	37·6
Second Masters and Mistresses						
Graduates	50·0‡	69·1	66·6	45·5	63·1	65·0
Total	68·0	71·7	69·7	60·0	70·8	70·4
Other Department Heads						
Graduates	37·6	24·6	28·7	18·7	17·9	23·4
Total	62·3	26·8	32·1	22·8	24·6	27·4
Scale 3 Posts						
Graduates	30·4	25·5	34·1	15·2	25·4	30·0
Total	53·3	27·5	36·7	20·0	26·8	30·8
Scale 2 Posts						
Graduates	29·6	36·9	37·3	31·1	33·4	35·7
Total	55·7	34·4	38·5	27·4	35·2	36·3
Scale 1 Posts						
Graduates	49·6	44·3	44·8	31·0	43·8	43·9
Total	69·8	42·4	45·3	28·6	42·6	43·1
Other Assistants						
Graduates	75·6	52·7	52·7	36·9	52·1	53·3
Total	87·5	55·6	54·2	40·3	54·7	57·8
All Teachers						
Graduates	60·2	36·3	38·5	26·3	32·5	36·3
Total	75·4	42·1	40·8	28·8	38·5	42·1
Total (000s)	(172·3)	(57·9)	(32·1)	(2·1)	(57·7)	(170·5)

*Full-time only.
†Including Nursery, and Middle deemed Primary.
‡Less than 10 posts in total.
§A further 2,850 divide their service between Primary and Secondary.

Source: Statistics of Education, 1971, Vol 4, Teachers (Table 20) (England and Wales

Appendix 17

Grade of teachers* in Further Education (grant aided)
at 31st March, 1971 (provisional)

Numbers in each grade (graduates and others)

Grade	Men	Women	Women as percent. of total
Principals			
Trained	269	20	6·9
Not Trained	386	12	3·0
Vice Principals (also department head)			
Trained	47	4	7·8
Not Trained	113	3	2·6
Vice Principals (not department heads)			
Trained	76	4	5·0
Not Trained	114	16	12·3
Other department heads			
Trained	704	143	16·9
Not Trained	1,414	64	4·3

*Full-time only.
Source: Statistics of Education, 1971, Vol 4, Teachers (Table 31)
(England and Wales).

Appendix 18

Qualifications of graduate teachers* in maintained primary and secondary schools at 31st March, 1971 (provisional)

Numbers with each qualification

Subject†	Primary		Secondary	
	Men	Women	Men	Women
Mathematics				
1 subject only	29	56	2,092	1,197
2 subjects including maths	89	75	2,237	704
3 subjects including maths	80	49	1,045	282
(Maths as first subject)	(132)	(124)	(3,893)	(1,773)
Physics				
1 subject only	20	13	1,465	283
2 subjects including physics	86	35	2,324	523
3 subjects including physics	62	12	930	160
(Physics as first subject)	(63)	(22)	(2,619)	(501)
Chemistry				
1 subject only	40	36	2,003	520
2 subjects including chemistry	48	58	1,303	466
3 subjects including chemistry	61	20	848	213
(Chemistry as first subject)	(83)	(74)	(3,097)	(844)

*Full-time only.
†Selected from the complete analysis.

Source: Statistics of Education, 1971, Vol 4, Teachers (Table 19) (England and Wales).

Appendix 19

**Qualifications of teachers* in Direct Grant Grammar Schools
at 31st March, 1971 (provisional)
Numbers with each qualification**

Qualification	Men	Women
Graduates		
Mathematics	281	200
Science†	651	372
Others	1,560	1,213
Total	2,492	1,785
Non-Graduates		
Trained	621	1,068
Not trained	381	438
Total	1,002	1,506
Overall Total	3,494	3,291

*Full-time only.
†Including Medicine, Technology and Agriculture.
Source: Statistics of Education, 1971, Vol 4, Teachers (Table 28)
(England and Wales).

Appendix 20

Qualifications of teachers* in Independent Schools (recognized as efficient) at 31st March, 1971 (provisional)

Numbers with each qualification

Qualification	Primary		Secondary		Primary/ Secondary	
	Men	Women	Men	Women	Men	Women
Graduates						
Mathematics	120	25	502	129	254	20
Science	108	34	906	201	539	32
Others	1,337	309	2,560	933	1,617	1,52
Total	1,565	368	3,968	1,263	2,410	2,05
Non-Graduates	1,708	2,818	804	771	822	2,68
Overall Total	3,273	3,186	4,772	2,034	3,232	4,74

*Full-time only.
Source: Statistics of Education, 1971, Vol 4, Teachers (Table 29), (England and Wales)

Appendix 21

**Qualifications of teachers* in further education
(grant aided) at 31st March 1971 (provisional)
Numbers with each qualification**

Qualification	Men	Women
Graduates		
Mathematics	1,526	164
Science (including medicine)	3,767	479
Technology	2,741	27
Agriculture	328	18
Other	7,252	1,787
Total	15,614	2,475
Non-Graduates	29,355	5,367
Overall Total	44,969	7,842

*Full-time only

Source: Statistics of Education, 1971, Vol 4. Teachers (table 30)
(England and Wales)

Appendix 22

**Grade and qualification of teachers* in colleges of Education
at 31st March, 1971 (provisional)**
Numbers in each grade

Qualification	Principals		Deputy Principals		Principal Lecturers	
	Men	Women	Men	Women	Men	Women
Graduates						
Mathematics	8	7	6	3	106	19
Science†	14	7	10	2	203	68
Others	49	43	52	43	753	241
Total	71	57	68	48	1,062	328
Non-Graduates						
Trained	9	11	12	17	410	213
Not Trained	2	10	2	6	114	107
Total	11	21	14	23	524	320
Overall Total	82	78	82	71	1,586	648

Qualification	All Grades	
	Men	Women
Graduates		
Mathematics	356	105
Science†	906	254
Others	3,240	1,146
Total	4,502	1,505
Non-Graduates		
Trained	2,261	1,530
Not trained	467	492
Total	2,728	2,022
Overall Total	7,230	3,527

*Full-time only.
†Including Medicine, Technology and Agriculture.

Source: Statistics of Education, 1971, Vol 4, Teachers (Table 35) (England and Wales)

Appendix 23

Numbers of women employees as percentage of total employed in the Engineering and Allied Industries* 1966, 1969 and 1972

Occupation	Women as percentage of Total Number			Total Number of Men & Women May, 1972
	May 1966	May 1969	May 1972	
Managers, Works Superintendents, Department Managers	2·8	2·5	2·3	191,255
Scientists and Technicians	1·6	1·8	1·2	58,845
Draughtsmen	1·5	1·4	0·9	75,210
Other Technicians	3·4	2·6	2·3	144,045
Clerical and Office Staff	59·0	59·3	60·0	408,265
Other Administrative, Technical and Commercial Staff	19·0	15·3	14·1	145,665
Total Administrative Technical and Clerical	30·5	28·1	26·8	1,023,285
Skilled Production Worker†	2·0	1·5	1·5	742,880
Skilled Maintenence Worker†	0·9	0·4	0·5	86,370
Other Production Worker‡	39·0	39·6	38·9	844,690
Foremen and Chargehands	4·4	5·1	6·1	47,145
Warehouse, Packers and Dispatch	18·1	18·4	16·4	130,245
Transport Drivers	1·2	0·9	1·2	34,685
Canteen Staff	90·6	90·8	91·0	24,025
Labourers	3·1	3·3	3·0	111,830
Other Manual	30·8	27·6	28·2	147,820
Total Manual	19·8	20·4	19·8	2,169,690
Overall Total	22·9	22·7	22·1	3,192,975

*In establishments employing 11 or more people.
†Normal method of entry by apprenticeship or equivalent training (apprentices and trainees are included).
‡Degree of skill acquired by some training and/or experience.

Source: Department of Employment *Gazette.*

Appendix 24

Analysis by industry and type of employment entered (1971) (percentages)

Industry	Apprentice Skilled Occupation		Employment leading to Professional Qualification		Clerical Employment		With Planned Training†		Other Employment		Total Numbers entering	
	Boys	Girls	Boys	Girls	Boys	Girls	Boys	Girls	Boys	Girls	Boys	Girls
Agriculture, Forestry, Fishing	13·9	4·9	0·1	0·5	0·4	13·5	11·7	12·7	73·9	68·4	12,070	1,669
Mining and Quarrying	58·0		0·4	2·2	2·2	82·8	32·4	4·9	7·0	10·1	4,808	227
Food, Drink and Tobacco	11·6	1·9	0·4	0·1	4·5	24·9	7·0	7·7	76·5	65·4	6,570	6,963
Coal and Petroleum products	62·5	2·8	3·8		8·3	79·8	14·4	4·9	11·0	12·5	264	144
Chemicals and Allied	37·7	1·8	2·2	1·1	7·7	46·3	17·9	10·4	34·5	40·4	2,177	3,255
Metal Manufacture	55·2	1·7	0·8	0·3	5·9	79·4	15·7	3·8	22·4	14·8	5,097	1,174
Mechanical Engineering	69·1	1·8	0·4	0·1	3·5	77·6	12·8	4·6	14·2	15·9	13,130	3,435
Instrument Engineering	46·1	1·0	0·5	0·4	4·0	51·8	26·6	13·4	22·9	33·4	1,389	931
Electrical Engineering	55·7	0·7	0·4	0·1	3·7	30·9	17·2	14·5	22·9	53·8	5,678	5,342
Shipbuilding and Marine Engineering	84·9	7·8	0·4	1·0	3·3	83·4	3·6	3·4	7·8	4·4	3,264	206
Vehicles	71·2	1·6	0·4	0·1	2·4	69·5	11·4	6·8	14·6	22·0	5,240	1,107
Metal Goods (n.e.s.)	41·0	0·8	0·5	0·1	2·8	50·0	21·8	7·9	34·0	41·2	10,614	3,641
Textiles	13·5	0·7	0·7	0·2	4·7	16·5	29·6	49·0	51·7	33·6	4,395	9,133
Leather, Leather Goods and Fur	10·6	1·4	0·4	0	2·0	16·7	32·1	38·5	54·6	43·4	898	789
Clothing and Footwear	11·1	0·8	0·4	0·1	3·4	5·2	44·2	63·3	40·9	30·6	4,050	22,745
Bricks, Pottery, Glass, Cement etc	23·5	0·8	0·7	0·2	7·2	47·1	19·3	25·2	49·6	26·7	2,655	1,531
Timber, Furniture etc.	28·4	1·4	0·2	0·9	2·2	50·9	21·6	11·5	47·6	35·3	7,365	1,528
Paper, Printing and Publishing	42·1	2·7	0·5	0·2	9·0	35·8	18·3	20·9	29·9	40·4	5,820	6,247
Other Manufacturing Industries	23·7	1·4	0·5	0·2	4·4	26·4	20·4	14·9	51·0	57·0	2,802	2,908
All Manufacturing Industries	43·3	1·2	0·5	0·2	4·2	26·9	18·2	33·6	33·8	38·1	81,408	71,709
Construction	65·9	2·0	0·7	0·1	2·5	90·7	8·4	2·0	22·5	5·2	30,872	2,834
Gas, Electricity and Water	75·3	1·3	0·9	0·4	16·6	91·2	4·0	3·8	3·2	3·3	2,796	1,417
Transport and Communications	43·3	1·4	1·3	0·3	20·2	72·3	15·4	19·7	19·8	6·3	9,174	5,152
Distributive Trades	12·7	1·2	0·3	0·1	4·1	20·4	17·7	10·4	65·2	67·9	45,085	64,593
Insurance, Banking, Financial and Business Services	7·4	0·2	5·9	0·7	74·0	96·1	5·9	1·6	6·8	1·4	5,168	18,603
Professional and Scientific Services	27·1	6·0	19·1	17·8	25·1	50·2	17·5	15·6	11·2	10·4	5,304	18,226
Miscellaneous Services	52·7	47·0	0·5	0·4	3·0	17·9	14·8	6·1	29·0	28·6	28,274	28,477
*Catering, Hotels, etc	36·4	5·0	0·7	0·4	1·6	12·8	20·4	10·9	40·9	70·9	5,474	5,307
*Motor Repairers, Garages, etc	65·7	2·8	0·1	0·8	2·4	79·7	13·0	2·3	18·8	14·4	16,792	2,470
*Hairdressing and Manicure	88·3	93·9	0·4	0·2	0·7	0·9	4·8	2·5	5·8	2·5	915	13,497
Public Administration and Defence	40·8	3·5	4·1	4·1	17·9	77·7	19·9	9·1	17·3	5·6	17,163	8,130
Overall Total	39·5	7·6	1·3	1·8	7·3	35·8	16·0	17·0	35·9	37·8	242,122	220,407

†Apart from induction training and training covered by other columns. *Included in Miscellaneous Services.

Appendix 25
Degree of Job Satisfaction

Working persons aged 15 or over who were less than 'very satisfied' with their job by sex by degree of job satisfaction by reasons for dissatisfaction

Great Britain

	Degree of Job Satisfaction				
Reason (Males)	Fairly satisfied	Neither satisfied nor dissatisfied	Rather dissatisfied	Very dissatisfied	Total
	%	%	%	%	%
Pay	36·0	38·3	44·8	50·3	37·7
Dissatisfied with administration/ organization	16·7	20·1	37·8	39·3	19·9
Did not like the kind of work	15·6	24·0	23·0	25·6	17·6
Physical working conditions	8·1	11·1	12·2	17·4	9·3
Heavy work	4·7	5·4	4·6	6·9	4·9
Lack of security	6·6	7·9	8·7	9·6	7·1
Long hours	4·0	4·7	5·7	8·7	4·4
Lack of opportunity	5·4	6·3	8·1	6·9	5·8
Shift work	4·5	5·9	5·2	5·1	4·7
Low status of work	3·4	4·0	7·0	4·6	3·8
Too much travelling (both to work and within work)	3·6	4·5	2·5	1·9	3·5
Too much responsibility	0·6	1·1	0·6	1·4	0·7
No real reason/don't know	13·0	7·4	0·6	Nil	10·7
Other reasons	7·8	6·7	4·9	6·0	7·3
BASE (=100%)	3,494	559	371	219	4,643
	%	%	%	No.	%
Reason (Females)					
Pay	22·5	24·4	21·1	(15)	22·6
Dissatisfied with administration/ organization	20·0	22·0	41·5	(23)	22·1
Did not like the kind of work	23·6	29·6	47·0	(30)	26·5
Physical working conditions	7·2	8·0	8·2	(9)	7·5
Heavy work	9·7	13·6	11·6	(8)	10·4
Lack of security	1·8	3·2	4·8	(Nil)	2·1
Long hours	6·1	5·6	7·5	(8)	6·3
Lack of opportunity	2·0	2·0	4·8	(1)	2·1
Shift work	2·2	3·2	2·8	(Nil)	2·3
Low status of work	3·5	5·6	4·8	(5)	4·0
Too much travelling (both to work and within work)	2·5	3·2	6·2	(4)	2·9
Too much responsibility	0·6	1·6	1·4	(2)	0·8
No real reason/don't know	14·1	9·6	0·7	(1)	12·3
Other reasons	6·5	8·4	6·8	(1)	6·6
BASE (=100%)	1,725	250	147	68	2,190

Source: General Household Survey, 1971. Introductory Report, 1973.

Appendix 26

Recommendations of the Departmental Committee, 1971

Recruitment
1   It should be open to both men and women to be considered for any job, and appointments should be solely on the grounds of suitability and qualifications.

Promotion
2   Wherever practicable, departments should arrange for promotion boards to consist of both men and women.

Marriage gratuity
3   Women who now qualify for a marriage gratuity should, under the new superannuation scheme, qualify for either deferred pension benefits or a short service gratuity.

Allowances
4   All rules governing Civil Service allowances should be examined with the intention of removing any discrimination on the grounds of sex.

Special leave to accompany husbands to new areas
5   Unpaid leave of up to three years should be available to a woman whose services her Department wishes to retain if she accompanies her husband on a move required by his employment to a place where she cannot continue her own employment in the Civil Service.

Annual leave
6   Departments should review their annual leave arrangements to ensure that so far as possible married women are able to take annual leave at the same time as their husbands.

Leave for urgent domestic affairs

7   Departments should use more widely their discretion in granting both paid and unpaid special leave for urgent domestic affairs; and it should be unnecessary first to exhaust annual leave.

Maternity leave

8   For established staff, paid maternity leave should be increased to three months, but entitlement to the third month's pay should depend upon three months' effective service having been given after return to work. Established staff should, in addition to the three months' paid leave, be entitled to up to three months' unpaid leave; departments should continue to have discretion to grant further unpaid leave and should consider applications for such leave sympathetically.

9   For unestablished staff with more than five years' service, paid maternity leave should be increased to six weeks, but entitlement to the final two weeks' pay should depend on three months' effective service having been given after return to work. Unestablished staff with more than five years' service should, in addition to six weeks' paid leave, be entitled to four-and-a-half months' unpaid leave; unestablished staff with less than five years' service should be entitled to six months' unpaid leave; departments should have discretion to grant additional unpaid leave to unestablished staff.

Part time work

10   Departments should examine the organization of their work and consider where appropriate part time work can be provided for serving or former women civil servants who are giving or have given satisfactory service, who are unable to work full time because they have children to care for, but who wish to continue or resume work in the Service. Departments which have a substantial amount of case work or a high turnover of staff or a large amount of

overtime or blocks of routine work should introduce part-time posts on an experimental basis.

Nurseries
11   At least one nursery should be set up for an experimental period of four years for the children of civil servants in an area other than London; fees should be fixed in relation to salary but with a maximum equivalent to economic cost; if the experiment proves to be of value to the Civil Service it should continue and other nurseries should be set up on a similar basis.

Unpaid leave for school holidays
12   Where work and staff holiday arrangements permit, departments should consider sympathetically applications from women who have children at school for some unpaid leave during school holidays, particularly where the applicant has only the basic leave allowance.

Flexibility of hours
13   Departments should encourage the use of discretion in arranging the hours of attendance of women with family responsibilities.

Unpaid leave after long service
14   Women who have children and who have had at least 20 years' service should be able to take at least six months' and not more than 12 months' unpaid leave, at a time to be agreed with the Department.

Elderly or infirm dependants or relatives
15   Where a woman has elderly or infirm dependants or relatives, departments should ensure that every effort is made to help her to cope with her domestic responsibilities while continuing her employment and, where appropriate, to provide a part time post for her; unpaid leave should be available if the dependant or relative requires considerable attention.

Reinstatement

16 Applicants for reinstatement should not be required to state their intention to remain permanently in the Service.

17 Women who resigned because of domestic responsibilities should not be debarred from reinstatement in grades up to and including the substantive grade held on resignation.

18 Rejection of an application for reinstatement to a specific grade should be made only at the level at which promotion to the grade concerned is confirmed.

19 A special competition on the lines of those held for regular members of the forces and members of Her Majesty's Overseas Civil Service should be held by the Civil Service Commission for former civil servants for reinstatement to the executive officer grade.

20 Where there are no vacancies in the former department in recruitment grades equivalent to, or higher than, executive officer, the applications should be considered by the Civil Service Commission alongside those of open competition candidates for those grades, without the age restrictions, if any, applicable to the latter.

21 On reinstatement, previous service should be taken into account in all cases in determining conditions of service, in particular starting salary and promotion seniority.

Training

22 Departments should, in consultation with the Civil Service Department, advise women who wish to prepare to return to work of the appropriate retraining.

23 As far as possible there should be flexible arrangements for the training of women who find it difficult to leave home to attend residential courses.

Information about conditions of service

24 Recruitment literature should explain what provisions there are to assist women to combine a family with a career in the Service; and departments should ensure that full

information is readily available to staff on the provisions for maternity leave, paid and unpaid leave for special reasons, reinstatement, and retraining.

Review of progress
25   There should be within two years of this Report a review of progress on the operation of those of our recommendations which are accepted; the Civil Service Department should consider how progress can best be monitored in the meantime.

Source: CSD Management Study No 3

Appendix 27

Recommendations of The House of Commons
Employment and Social Services Sub-Committee

1 That a concentrated effort should be made through careers guidance to make girls aware of the range of employment opportunities available to them.

2 That the provision of day-release for young workers should be made a statutory requirement on all employers.

3 That commercial apprenticeships should be provided for young workers in clerical work.

4 That the impact on training of the reduced levy of 1 per cent should be closely monitored.

5 That the inequality in the training grants paid to men and women should be removed.

6 That consideration should be given to the organization of work so that flexible working hours and the choice between full and part time work can be made available to the maximum number of women.

7 The rapid expansion of day nurseries and nursery school provision with flexible hours adjusted to the requirements of working mothers.

8 The provision of facilities for the after-school and holiday care of school age children.

9 That the DE should have regular contact with women's organizations and particularly with the Women's National Commission.

10 That play areas be provided in employment exchanges.

11 That officers with specialist knowledge of the matters most closely affecting women at work should be available to give advice in Jobcentres.

12 That as soon as employment exchanges are in a position

to accept and process the information there should be a statutory requirement to notify all vacancies to the State employment offices.

13 DE to undertake an enquiry into the conditions under which home work is carried out, to obtain reliable figures on the evasion of registration, and to ensure that this registration is properly enforced in the future.

14 That consideration should be given to the possibility of increasing the 'disregard' of £2 or basing the size of 'disregard' on the number of dependants.

15 That DE should bear in mind the local availability of labour when considering whether work permits should be granted.

Appendix 28

Days lost through absence

Working persons aged 15 or over by age and sex, percentage of each group absent from work in the reference week subdivided by reasons for absence.

Age	Own illness/accident			Holiday*			Strike/short time/lay-off			Personal and other reasons			Total Absent			BASE (=100%) all persons working		
	M	F	T	M	F	T	M	F	T	M	F	T	M	F	T	M	F	T
15—17%	6·1	4·4	5·2	7·5	7·2	7·2	0·7	0·3	0·4	1·5	1·5	1·4	15·6	13·4	14·2	411	390	801
18—24%	5·5	7·4	6·3	9·5	9·8	9·6	0·7	0·7	0·7	1·6	1·8	1·6	17·3	19·7	18·2	1,354	957	2,310
25—34%	4·2	5·7	4·6	10·1	12·9	11·0	0·8	0·3	0·6	1·4	2·6	1·8	16·5	21·5	18·0	1,966	919	2,884
35—44%	4·3	3·8	4·1	10·7	11·8	11·1	0·9	1·1	1·0	1·0	1·0	1·0	16·9	17·8	17·2	1,978	1,228	3,206
45—54%	4·7	4·3	4·5	10·6	11·8	11·1	0·7	1·1	0·9	0·7	1·2	0·9	16·7	18·4	17·4	1,993	1,310	3,302
55—64%	6·5	4·6	5·9	9·7	11·9	10·4	0·8	0·4	0·6	0·9	1·2	1·0	17·9	18·1	17·9	1,591	826	2,416
65+%	3·9	4·3	4·1	11·6	6·2	9·6	1·2	Nil	0·7	1·6	Nil	1·0	18·3	10·5	15·4	258	161	418
Total %	5·0	5·0	5·0	10·1	11·2	10·5	0·8	0·7	0·7	1·1	1·4	1·2	17·0	18·3	17·4	9,549	5,789	15,338

*Excluding public holidays.

Source: General Household Survey, 1971. Introductory Report, 1973.

Appendix 29

LENGTH OF ABSENCE

Working persons aged 15 or over absent from work in the reference week by sex and reasons for absence by length of absence

Great Britain

Length of Absence from Work	Own illness/ accident			Holiday*			Strike/ Short time/ Lay-off			Personal or other reasons			Total Absent		
	M	F	T	M	F	T	M	F	T	M	F	T	M	F	T
	%	%	%	%	%	%	No.	No.	%	%	No.	%	%	%	%
Less than 1 week	46·2	57·7	50·6	52·0	53·1	52·4	(48)	(24)	63·4	89·2	(71)	88·5	53·3	57·3	54·7
1 week but less than 2	17·2	14·1	15·9	25·6	23·1	24·6	(11)	(6)	14·3	5·9	(3)	4·9	21·4	18·9	20·4
2 weeks but less than 4	13·1	10·9	12·2	20·3	19·8	20·1	(5)	(5)	8·9	4·9	(4)	4·9	16·6	16·0	16·3
4 weeks but less than 13	15·9	14·4	15·4	2·0	3·9	2·8	(9)	(5)	12·5	Nil	(2)	1·1	6·4	7·0	6·6
13 weeks or more	7·5	3·2	5·9	0·1	Nil	0·1	(1)	(Nil)	0·9	Nil	(1)	0·5	2·3	1·0	1·8
BASE (=100%)	465	284	747	952	640	1,592	74	40	112	102	81	182	1,593	1,045	2,638

*Excluding public holidays.

Source: General Household Survey, 1971. Introductory Report, 1973.

Appendix 30

Equal Pay Act, 1970
A brief summary of the main provisions.

1 The title

Although this is called the "Equal Pay Act" it is concerned with more than "pay". Its purpose is to require "equal treatment as regards terms and conditions of employment to men and to women" "of whatever age" in certain circumstances. (Clauses 1(1) and 11(2)).

2 The circumstances affected

2.1 Where men and women are employed on "like work", ie "of the same or broadly similar nature" and where any differences between the things done "are not of practical importance in relation to terms and conditions of employment". (Clauses 1(1) (a) and 1(4)).

2.2 Where their work is "rated as equivalent", ie "given an equal value, in terms of the demand made on a worker under various headings (for instance, effort, skill, decision)" or "would have been given an equal value but for the evaluation being made on a system setting different values for men and women on the same demand under any heading". (Clauses 1(1) (b) and 1(5)).

2.3 Any "collective agreement" containing "any provision applying specifically to men only or to women only" may be referred to the Industrial Arbitration Board" to declare what amendments need to be made" to "remove that discrimination between men and women". Such amendments must not extend the operation of the agreement to men or women not previously covered by it. (Clauses 3(1) to (5)).

2.4 Any "employer's pay structure", ie "any arrangements adopted by an employer which fix common terms and conditions of employment for his employees or any class of his employees, and of which the provisions are generally known or open to be known by the employees concerned" may also be referred to the Industrial Arbitration Board to declare amendments. (Clauses 3(6) and (7)).

2.5 A Wages Regulation Order made under the Wages Councils Act or the Agricultural Wages Act may similarly be referred. (Clauses 4 and 5).

3 Definition of 'Same Employment'

A woman must be given equal treatment with men "in the same employment", ie with "men employed by her employer or any associated employer at the same establishment or at establishments in Great Britain which include that one and at which common terms and conditions of employment are observed either generally or for employees of the relevant classes". (Clauses 1(2) and 1(6)).

4 Exceptions

The requirement of equal treatment does not apply in so far as the terms and conditions of a woman's employment are affected by compliance with legal restrictions, by special treatment in connection with child-bearing, or by the terms and conditions related to retirement, marriage or death. (Clause 6).

5 Commencement

5.1 The provisions come into force on the 29 December 1975. (Clause 9(1)).

5.2 " . . . to secure orderly progress towards equal treatment" the Secretary of State could have required, by order, that, on 31 December 1973, any differences in treatment were subject to a limitation and that the rate paid to a woman should not be less than nine-tenths (or a higher fraction) of the rate paid to men with whom equal treatment was required by the Act. (Clauses 9(2) and (3)).

5.3 A collective agreement, pay structure or wages order may be referred to the Industrial Arbitration Board during 1975 to declare what amendments need to be made (Clauses 10(1), (2) and (3)).

5.4 If an order had been made imposing a limitation on differences with effect from 31 December 1973, then collective agreements, pay structures or wages orders could have been referred to the Industrial Arbitration Board, during the year before that to declare what amendments needed to be made to meet that order. (Clause 10(4)).

6 Enforcement

6.1 Any claim (based on Clause 1 of the Act) for alteration of a term or condition of employment or for arrears of pay or for damages may be referred to and determined by an Industrial Tribunal. The reference may be made by an individual (employee or employer) or by the Secretary of State. (Clauses 2(1), (2) and (3)).

6.2 A claim will not be valid if the woman "has not been employed in the employment within the six months preceding the date of the reference". (Clause 2(4)).

6.3 Arrears awarded by the Tribunal may not exceed a period of two years. (Clause 2(5)).

6.4 In the event of a claim for equal treatment for a woman (or man), employed in circumstances where an Industrial Tribunal decides that equal treatment with a man (or woman) is required by the Act, the onus is on the employer to show that any advantage enjoyed by the man (or woman) is not due to the difference of sex. (Clause 2(6)).

Armed forces and police pay

These matters are covered by Clauses 7 and 8.

205

Appendix 31

Analysis of incomes by age group (Graduates only)

Percentages

Income per annum	All Ages W	All Ages M	Under 25 W	Under 25 M	25–29 W	25–29 M	30–34 W	30–34 M	35–39 W	35–39 M	40–44 W	40–44 M	45–49 W	45–49 M	50 and over W	50 and over M
Below £1,000	3·0	0·6	7·6	4·2	2·3	1·1	1·6	0·2	1·0	<0·1	1·7	<0·1	—	—	1·3	0·3
£1,000	4·6	0·7	16·9	5·5	1·8	0·9	0·8	0·1	—	0·1	—	—	—	—	0·7	0·2
£1,200	12·1	3·0	35·8	29·7	14·1	3·1	4·0	0·4	1·0	<0·1	—	0·1	—	—	—	0·2
£1,400	12·1	4·5	25·7	31·6	24·6	10·2	0·8	0·9	2·0	0·1	4·2	0·3	1·2	0·1	—	0·4
£1,600	10·7	5·4	10·0	17·4	25·0	20·3	11·9	2·5	7·0	0·5	5·9	0·7	1·2	0·2	2·0	0·4
£1,800	8·3	5·7	3·2	6·8	15·4	21·5	16·7	5·9	7·0	1·7	5·9	8·1	8·5	0·6	2·0	0·6
£2,000	20·0	16·6	0·8	4·1	16·4	32·9	34·5	36·1	37·0	16·4	28·6	18·6	24·4	5·3	24·3	5·0
£2,500	14·8	17·9	—	0·5	0·5	7·8	23·0	35·4	34·0	31·4	21·0	40·1	30·5	14·0	27·0	11·2
£3,000	10·0	22·9	—	0·2	—	2·0	5·6	16·5	8·0	36·7	28·6	19·4	23·2	31·2	24·3	26·2
£4,000	3·6	11·2	—	—	—	<0·1	0·8	1·1	3·0	8·2	1·7	12·6	11·0	24·1	15·1	22·2
£5,000 and over	0·8	11·5	—	—	—	0·1	—	0·9	—	4·8	2·5	—	—	—	3·3	32·8
Totals (000S)	(1·05)	(19·02)	(0·25)	(1·51)	(0·22)	(3·25)	(0·13)	(2·90)	(0·10)	(2·80)	(0·12)	(2·88)	(0·82)	(2·27)	(0·15)	(3·42)

Source: The Survey of Professional Scientists, 1971. (Department of Trade and Industry), (HMSO, 1973).

List of abbreviations

CBI	Confederation of British Industry
CNAA	Council for National Academic Awards
DES	Department of Education and Science
DHSS	Department of Health and Social Security
DITB	Distributive Industry Training Board
EEC	European Economic Community
EEF	Engineering Employers' Federation
EEOC	Equal Employment Opportunities Commission (USA)
EOC	Equal Opportunities Commission
GCE	General Certificate of Education
GMWU	General and Municipal Workers Union
HNC	Higher National Certificate
HND	Higher National Diploma
IDS	Incomes Data Services
ILO	International Labour Office
IMS	Institute of Manpower Studies
ITB	Industrial Training Board
NHS	National Health Service
NPD	Normal Pension Date
OECD	Organization for Economic Cooperation and Development
PEP	Political and Economic Planning
TUC	Trades Union Congress
UN	United Nations
USDAW	Union of Shop, Distributive and Allied Workers

Bibliography

Education, Training and Employment of Women and Girls, Association of Teachers in Technical Institutions, 1973

Employment of Women, Final Report of Regional Trade Union Seminar, Organization for Economic Cooperation and Development (OECD), 1968

Equal Pay, Report No 184, Industrial Society, 1973

FOGARTY M, *et al*, *Women in Top Jobs*, Political and Economic Planning (PEP), 1972

GAVRON H, *The Captive Wife*, Penguin, 1970

HUTT C, *Males and Females*, Penguin, 1972

Industrial Relations Review and Report, No 69, December 1973

Industrial Relations Review and Report, No 70, December 1973

Maternity Leave, Study No 58, Incomes Data Services (IDS), August 1973

MEPHAM G J, *Problems of Equal Pay*, Institute of Personnel Management (IPM), 1969

New Patterns for Working Time, Report of International Conference, OECD, 1972

NIVEN M, *Personnel Management 1913–63*, IPM, 1967

Participation of Women in the Economic and Social Development in their Countries, United Nations, 1970

Part-time work, Study No 62, IDS, October 1973

PINDER P, *Women at Work*, PEP, 1969

Women's Pay, Study No 56, IDS, July 1973

WYNN M, *Family Policy*, Penguin, 1972

YOUNG M and WILMOTT P, *The Symmetrical Family*, Routledge and Kegan Paul, 1973

Government publications

Census 1971, Summary Tables (1 per cent sample), HMSO, 1973

Education Statisticts for the UK, Department of Education and Science (DES), 1971

Employment of Women in the Civil Service, Civil Service Department Management Study No 3, HMSO ,1971

Equal Opportunities for Men and Women, Department of Employment (DE), 1973

Equal Pay, A guide to the Equal Pay Act 1970, DE, 1971

Equal Pay, First report on implementation of the Equal Pay Act, Office of Manpower Economics (OME), 1972

Equal Pay, What are you doing about it? DE, 1973

Female Activity Rates, *DE Gazette*, January 1974

General Household Survey 1971, HMSO, 1973

Government Observations on Expenditure Committee Reports, 1972–3, Cmnd 5536, HMSO, 1973

HUNT A, *Survey of Women's Employment*, Ministry of Labour, 1968

Minutes of Evidence and Proceedings of the House of Lords Select Committee on the Anti-Discrimination Bill (HL), 1971–72, SBN 10 416072 1, HMSO, 1972

Minutes of Evidence and Proceedings of the House of Lords Select Committee on the Anti-Discrimination Bill (HL), 1972–3, SBN 10 401373 7, HMSO, 1973

Monopolies Commission Report on the Supply of Professional Services, Cmnd 4463, HMSO, 1970

Second Special Report from the House of Lords Select Committee on the Anti-Discrimination Bill (HL). 1972–3, SBN 10 410473 2, HMSO, 1973

SEEAR N, *The Position of Women in Industry*, HMSO, 1968

Sixth Report from the House of Commons Expenditure Committee (with minutes of evidence and proceedings of the Employment and Social Services Sub-Committee) on the Employment of Women, 1972–3, SBN 10 218273 6, HMSO, 1973

Special Report from the House of Commons Select Committee on the Anti-Discrimination (No 2) Bill, 1972–3, SBN 10 233373 4, HMSO, 1973

Statistics of Education (England and Wales), DES, 1971

Survey of Professional Scientists 1971, Department of Trade and Industry, 1973

IPM Publishing

Management Paperbacks
Management in Perspective
Handbooks
Surveys

Four series with something to interest *you*. Write for a free copy of our full catalogue: new titles are added regularly. Some of our publications are described overleaf.

IPM Courses and Conferences

A comprehensive programme of courses, seminars and conferences, ranging from basic procedures to the latest technique and development, is run throughout the year. The autumn National Conference is the largest management conference in the UK. Other major events are the annual London spring conference and the biennial International conference which attracts delegates from all over the world.

For a free catalogue or course and conference calendar, please write to IPM at the address on the title page.

The Practice of Personnel Management

by David Barber

A firm's personnel policy must be an integral part of overall company policy: it should therefore be its aim to develop an effective organization structure, man it with suitable people, and ensure that employees have the opportunity to make their best contribution. This basic publication emphasizes points of concern to the newcomer to personnel management but is equally one which every personnel manager should read. Chapter headings include corporate planning, organization structure, manpower planning and development, remuneration, and employee relations and services.

"As a manual of instruction it covers a wide range of personnel activities with great clarity ... well written and informative..."

British Journal of Industrial Relations

"Easy to read and a sound guide to modern practice."

The Supervisor

60p; 50p IPM members; 25p IPM students

Personnel Management in Hospitals

by Graham Millard

"Any departmental head reading this book will obtain a good background briefing on 1974, the Industrial Relations Act 1971, disciplinary and appeals procedures, productivity and bonus schemes. More important, he or she would be made aware of techniques they could adopt and implement themselves in things like interviewing, selection, induction communications and delegation".

The Hospital and Health Service Review

£1·25; £1·00 IPM members

Coming to Terms with Trade Unions

by W E J McCarthy and A S Collier

This book is about the nature of the challenge which trade unionism presents to management and the steps which management has to take to deal with it.

Six case studies show how ways of dealing with employees are found to be increasingly inappropriate as unions gain recognition and extend collective bargaining in a given firm or industry. The emphasis throughout is on strategy rather than tactics, on the questions that need to be answered if trade union-management relations are to be improved and adapted to fit changing circumstances over the medium and long term.

£1·25; 80p IPM members